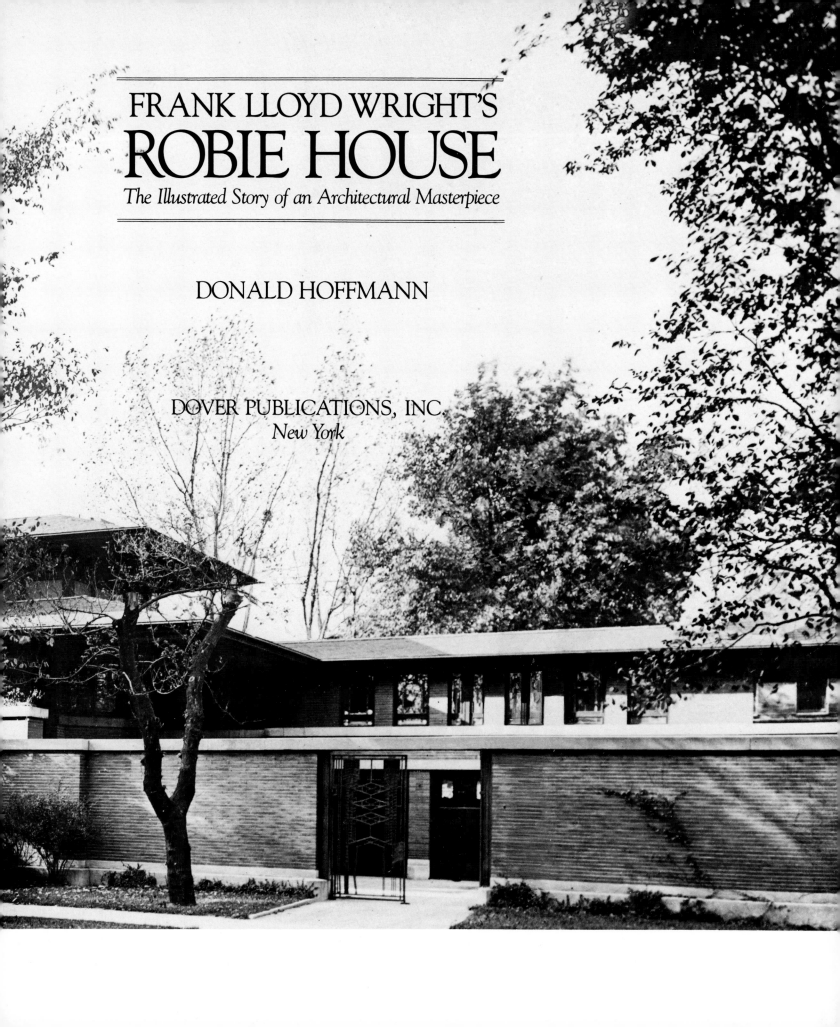

FRANK LLOYD WRIGHT'S
ROBIE HOUSE

The Illustrated Story of an Architectural Masterpiece

DONALD HOFFMANN

DOVER PUBLICATIONS, INC.
New York

Published in Canada by General Publishing Company, Ltd., 30 Lesmill Road, Don Mills, Toronto, Ontario.
Published in the United Kingdom by Constable and Company, Ltd.

Frank Lloyd Wright's Robie House: The Illustrated Story of an Architectural Masterpiece is a new work, first published by Dover Publications, Inc., in 1984.

Manufactured in the United States of America
Dover Publications, Inc., 31 East 2nd Street, Mineola, N.Y. 11501

Book design by Carol Belanger Grafton

Library of Congress Cataloging in Publication Data

Hoffmann, Donald.
  Frank Lloyd Wright's Robie House.

  Includes index.
  1. Robie House (Chicago, Ill.)   2. Chicago (Ill.)—Dwellings.   3. Wright, Frank Lloyd 1867–1959.   4. Organic architecture—Illinois—Chicago.   I. Title.
  NA7238.C4H63   1984   728.8'3'0924   83-7227
  ISBN 0-486-24582-9

ACKNOWLEDGMENTS

The house that was built in Chicago for Fred C. Robie is all too familiar as an image and not at all known as a reality. It still stands, but I would not wish to argue that it still truly exists. Because the house today cannot claim to be the primary document of its own history, I have cast parts of this study in the present tense and have prepared many illustrations to rebuild in the mind what has been lost to direct experience. This required the help of many persons. First came Lorraine Robie O'Connor, who left her father's house when only 16 months old. Today she is a most direct and alert woman; and it was my good fortune to discover also that for many years she has been an acquaintance of my mother's. Mrs. O'Connor was quick to share her invaluable collection of family documents. Phillips Taylor lived in the house as a young lad for nearly a year. His memories have proved as accurate as they are vivid. The late Jeannette Wilber Scofield, who had lived in the house from the time when she was six until she was 20, was a woman of great spirit and kindness. She helped me in every possible way, even into her last months.

Richard Twiss has been extraordinarily generous in providing encouragement and information. Hanna Holborn Gray, the president of the University of Chicago, unhesitatingly assured me of the university's cooperation. In expressing my gratitude to her, to Peter Kountz, who served as a dedicated curator of the Robie house, and to Carl F. Chapman, Rolf Achilles, Rudy Bernal, Calvert Audrain, Michael Boos, M. H. Sullivan and the staff of the university library, I must add that the university, which came to own the house with obvious reluctance, neither initiated nor sponsored this study. It remains one of the ironies of academic life that generations of students were introduced to art history through photographic reproductions while a very great work of art, next to the campus, was allowed to decay and nearly to vanish.

For their many kinds of help, I thank especially Hermann Pundt, Kenneth Breisch, Curtis Besinger, Robert Kostka, James O'Gorman, Buford Pickens, Jack Quinan, Leonard Eaton, William A. Storrer, Terry Marvel, W. B. Barnard, Joseph T. Dye, Maya Moran, Jean Green, Kathy Roy Cummings, John Vinci, Tim Samuelson, Janet Cyrwus, Tim Barton, Donald Kalec, Walter A. Netsch, Edgar Tafel, Charles Montooth, Bruce Brooks Pfeiffer, Holmes Knaus, Wolfgang Ritschka, Henry Klumb, Adolf Placzek, Irma Robie, Richard L. Tooke, John Zukowsky, Joseph Benson, Kathryn Smith and Valerie Hoffmann, my daughter. George Hoffmann and Alan Hoffmann, two of my sons, made Hyde Park a good place to visit. Edgar Kaufmann, jr., and John Hoffmann, both fine historians, were so kind as to read the manuscript and make helpful suggestions. I am very grateful, too, to the American Council of Learned Societies and to the Graham Foundation for Advanced Studies in the Fine Arts, which supported my research with grants.

D.H.

CONTENTS

LIST OF ILLUSTRATIONS

FRANK LLOYD WRIGHT'S
ROBIE HOUSE

Chapter I
FROM CLIENT TO ARCHITECT

Fred C. Robie liked to ride around Chicago, the city where he was born, in an experimental motorcar of his own making. It was streamlined and snappy, a more sensible car than most of those on the streets today. If the "Robie Cycle Car," as he called it, never quite got into production, at least it said that its owner chose not to be taken as an ordinary man [Fig. 1]. Robie had every reason to think that he was going places. His new house in Hyde Park looked very much as if it might be, too [2]. It was sure to be seen someday as a consummate expression of the ideas and ideals of its architect, Frank Lloyd Wright. It was destined to be one of the most famous houses of America and one of the most famous houses of the twentieth century, anywhere.

Wright had come into his own a few years earlier, just at the turn of the century. The calendar itself must have cried out to such a radical spirit for full proof of good works in the cause of modernism. In 1902 a young man named Francis Barry Byrne went to work for Wright in his Oak Park studio, at the west edge of the city. Byrne stayed until the summer of 1908, not long before Wright planned the house for Robie. As an old man, Byrne loved to look back to that time:

> The years I worked under Frank Lloyd Wright were those which saw the emergence of that greatest of his contributions to a living architecture, a unique, vital, and relevant building plan which was to become a source factor in European modernism, and the unification of this vital plan with an equally vital building mass and detail. It was a period which marked the passing from his work of Sullivanesque remnants and the appearance of his own uniquely beautiful architecture in relative completeness.

ABOVE: 1. Fred C. Robie (left) in his experimental car, about 1906–1907. OPPOSITE: 2. Robie's house at 5757 Woodlawn Avenue, Chicago.

> The culmination of this happy period in his life as an architect was the Robie house.[1]

Wright stretched the house low to the ground. Each stroke of the design he made as decisive as could be, bringing every detail into line, so that the house would gain that integrity of character which amounts to true style. Surely the time was ripe for a robust mind to

---

[1] Barry Byrne, rev. of *The Drawings of Frank Lloyd Wright*, the *Journal of the Society of Architectural Historians (JSAH)*, XXII (May 1963), p. 109. Wright himself favored the house for Mr. and Mrs. Avery Coonley; their site in suburban Riverside, Ill., had allowed him to plan on the scale of a Roman villa, and as clients the Coonleys were more overtly spiritual.

respond to all the promises of modernism, untroubled by doubt and undiminished by irony.[2]

Frederick Carlton Robie was an only child who grew to have only one ambition, to be "a great manufac-

turer."[3] He was born August 14, 1879, and named for his paternal grandfather, who had been born in Germany and whose surname was originally Räbe. It is said in the family that the name got changed by a clerk in America who was unable to understand his German. Grandfather Robie ran a boot and shoe shop in Walworth, N.Y., where his son, George T. Robie, was born in 1853. George Robie arrived in Chicago a few years after the Great Fire of 1871. He worked as a salesman, married Anna Snook in 1877, and started the Excelsior Supply Company to market sewing-machine supplies.[4] Quick to

[2]"The average of human intelligence rises steadily," Wright declared in his first "In the Cause of Architecture" essay, the *Architectural Record*, XXIII (March 1908), p. 158. Only months before World War II, and in London, he could still speak of "these great opportunities now for the first time given to humanity by science, resulting in this gorgeous sense of speed and space." See *An Organic Architecture* (London, 1939), p. 17.

[3]Robie's words and those of his son are taken directly from two extraordinary tape recordings made early in 1958. Douglas Haskell, the editor of the *Architectural Forum*, asked for their memories of the house. Fred Robie, jr., who lived in Cherokee, N.C., took the request as an opportunity to visit his father in Cleveland, where he made one recording for Haskell's use and then a second concerning the tragedy of his father's business career. The *Forum* version of the first conversation ("Mr. Robie knew what he wanted," Oct. 1958, pp. 126*ff.*), often cited and republished, is not an authentic document; it is much excerpted and heavily edited. Lorraine Robie O'Connor kindly allowed me to transcribe both tapes.

[4]According to a printed memorial, George T. Robie arrived in Chicago in 1873 and established his company in 1876; city directories, however, do not list him until 1876–1877, or his company until 1884.

ABOVE: *3. Robie (far left) as captain of the "Orient Sextette," June 1897.* LEFT: *4. Ferris Wheel at the World's Columbian Exposition of 1893. The Gothic-style building at left is Foster Hall.* OPPOSITE: *5. Fred C. Robie and Lora Hieronymus, 1902.*

take advantage of new markets, he branched into the bicycle business in the 1880s. "He didn't go to school," Fred C. Robie told his own son, "and I didn't do much of it. So we didn't steal any honors or anything else in the educational line. That was good practical stuff—experience—we had."

When he was 16, in September 1895, Fred C. Robie entered the school of mechanical engineering at Purdue University. He left in February 1899, without earning a degree. He already had been selling bicycles, as he noted later on the back of a photograph of himself as captain of the "Orient Sextette" [3]:

> While at Purdue University, Lafayette, Indiana, I sold bicycles, Orient and others, for additional income. As an advertising stunt the Sextette was shipped to me and it created much interest among the students. Later this group took it to Indianapolis . . . and nearby towns to put on shows.

Robie returned to Chicago to work with his father, whom he greatly admired. "He was a background and a bulwark," Robie said nearly 60 years later, "and probably no other young man had finer." He lived with his parents in their Queen Anne–style house at 7124 Yale Avenue, in Englewood, about eight miles south of the business center of the city. He was at a dance at the University of Chicago when he met Lora Hieronymus. Her paternal ancestors also were Germans. Lora had been born May 14, 1878, in Pekin, Illinois. Her family had moved in 1886 to Springfield, the state capital, where her father, Benjamin R. Hieronymus, was later to become president of the Illinois National Bank. In 1893, when she was 15, Lora had gone with her father to Chicago to see the World's Columbian Exposition. On the Midway Plaisance they had ridden the giant Ferris Wheel, still another new and wondrous form of motion. Lora had looked down to see the new buildings of the university. The closest was Foster Hall, the women's dormitory on Lexington Avenue (later called University Avenue) at Fifty-ninth Street [4]. Lora said she would like to go to college there. And she did, beginning in 1896; and she lived in Foster Hall.

After she graduated in June 1900, Lora Hieronymus returned to Springfield and shortly began teaching ninth grade at the Lawrence School. Robie continued to court her. They were married at her home on June 30, 1902, by the minister of the Disciples of Christ Church she had attended in Hyde Park, near the university [5]. At first, Robie and his bride lived with his parents in Englewood; but by 1904 they had moved to an apartment in the

south wing of the Colonial Court, a brick building with stone quoins, Georgian in style and wholly characteristic of Hyde Park. It still stands at 5310–5312 Cornell Avenue, only half a block from the commuter rails that brought Hyde Park and Kenwood into being. By 1907, the elder Robies had taken rooms in the Windermere Hotel, three blocks south.[5] Fred Robie, jr., was born February 19, 1907. By the spring of 1908, Robie and his wife were planning to build their own house.

Robie was only 28, but he could entertain thoughts of an expensive residence; he was already sharing in the profits of his father's businesses and he was flirting with some of his own. He was especially interested in manufacturing motorcycles and his experimental cycle car:[6]

> My father refused to be a part of any manufacturing activity that I wanted to take over, except on a loan basis—not as a fixed investment. He was smart, smarter than hell. He got rid of the headaches of manufacturing, got rid of the financing of problematical changes in design, and he passed those on to the younger shoulders. . . . I was losing my interest in the bicycle business. I never had very much interest, except one of helpfulness, in the sewing-machine supply business. So we decided the manufacturing business would be an entirely separate organization.

---

[5]The residential hotel stood at the northwest corner of Fifty-sixth and Cornell. It was known later as the Windermere West, in deference to a newer Windermere Hotel across Cornell Avenue. The older hotel, built for the 1893 fair, was demolished in 1959.

[6]Robie makes clear that the logical development led from bicycles to motorcycles to cars (the differences then being comparatively slight). He dated his prototype car to 1906–1907 and described it as having a 90-inch wheelbase with seven-and-one-half-inch clearance, 28-inch tires and an air-cooled, four-cycle, two-cylinder engine. A later version was described in the *Automobile* of April 9, 1914, p. 779, as having "a unique streamline body design," a V-motor with two air-cooled cylinders, 108-inch wheelbase and weight of only 540 pounds. The *Motor World* of Aug. 19, 1914, p. 35, reported that 565 light cars were to be built by the Robie Motor Car Co. of Detroit for sale in England. The venture evidently was a casualty of World War I.

Well, my father's business prospered and mine prospered—large sums of money per year. . . . The Excelsior Company, the supply company, had been making an overall profit. . . . The bicycle business had always been profitable, and that of course was still growing at this time. The automobile-supply business seemed to indicate a field in which the Excelsior Company could well make a profit . . . ; this accessory store was established on Michigan Avenue, in the heart of a group of automotive supply manufacturers. . . . I had been enjoying a pretty lucrative salary, because the profits were split by us once a year, my father and I.

Robie found a site at the northeast corner of Fifty-eighth Street and Woodlawn Avenue. It was a little more than a mile from his apartment, and only two blocks from Foster Hall [6–8]. "My mother . . . was still interested in the campus life and the social life of the university," said Fred Robie, jr., "and father thought it would be a good idea to have a house within easy access of that atmosphere." Robie himself preferred to say only that a friend owned the house to the north: "His property was

very well cared for, he was a nut on flowers and so on, and I thought he'd make a good neighbor." Herbert E. Goodman, who lived at 5753 Woodlawn, was the general manager of a company that manufactured mining machinery. He and his wife Jennie had been investing in South Side real estate, and when they heard that a speculator hoped to build a storefront at 5757 Woodlawn, they bought the corner site to protect their own house. In a covenant of April 8, 1908, Robie agreed to build nothing but a residence. He bought the site on May 19 for $13,500.[7]

---

[7]Legally, the site is described as lot 16 and the south ten feet of lot 17 in block 71 of Gray & Gaylord's subdivision of block 71 and the west half of block 62 of Hopkin's addition to Hyde Park, a subdivision of the west half of the northeast quarter of Section 14, Township 38, Range 14, Cook County, Ill. The chain of title can be traced in ledger book 353-A, p. 219, Cook County Recorder of Deeds, and in the Recorder's microfiche library. An undated note in the files of the Chicago Theological Seminary says that the Goodmans "were horrified" by the prospect of a store and paid $10,000 for the corner site to prevent it. Later known as "Fensham House," to honor the first woman to have been graduated from the seminary, the Goodman house finally was demolished in 1958 for a new dormitory building.

BELOW: 6. *The house (shaded, center) in relation to major buildings of the University of Chicago, 1909–1910.* RIGHT: 7. *The university and the Midway Plaisance, 1907. The future site of the house is at center, in a dark mass of trees. Woodlawn Avenue crosses the Midway in the middle distance. Lake Michigan is at the horizon.* OPPOSITE, TOP: 8. *Looking east on Fifty-ninth Street, with Woodlawn Avenue at the first intersection. Blaine Hall (center) is at Kimbark Avenue.*

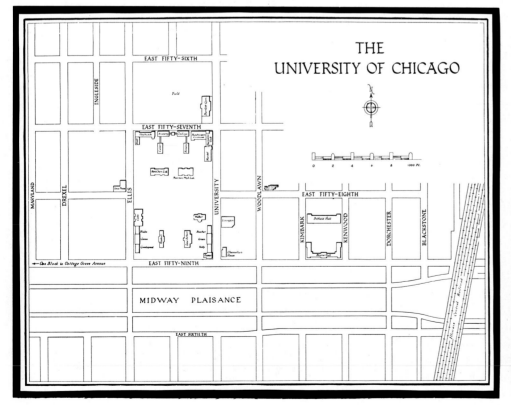

THE UNIVERSITY OF CHICAGO

What did he have in mind for a house? It is hard to be sure, because he told this story 50 years later:[8]

> In my original thoughts of the house, I definitely wanted it as nearly as possible—as a main feature—that it be made of materials that would be fireproof, and of such construction that the relationships of the rooms would be as—let me say—without interruption, long hallways, stairwells, and box-like partitions.

In other words, asked his son, he wanted to avoid what was prevalent?

> That's right. The idea of most of those houses was a kind of conglomeration of architecture . . . and they were absolutely cut up inside. They were drafty because they had great big stairwells [which] occupied a lot of very valuable space, interfering with outside window-gazing. I wanted no part of that.
>
> The layouts that I provided were gradually shaped-up to something that I could introduce to an architect, because I had no conception of construction, or design of an exterior of brick and gray sandstone trim, which I had in mind.
>
> I wanted the windows without curvatures and doodads, both inside and out. I wanted all the light I could get in the house, and shaded enough by overhanging eaves . . . somewhat protective of our views. In other words, I could sit—as I laid it ultimately out—I could sit across the room and look out in three different directions. . . . And most interesting were, possibly, the storms we had. Most perfect, from the health standpoint, was the excess light and beautiful suns of the summer . . . shaded, without direct sunlight, on open porches, and these porches to be outside on the south, because of the sun. . . . I could have sunlight into my living rooms in the morning, before I really went to work.
>
> I wanted this room to be so that I could look out to the north and see down the street to my neighbors, without their being able to invade *my* privacy. In some cases they had used a lot of fabrics and draperies and whatnot, including old-fashioned roller shades with the brass fittings on the ends, and a lot of other odds and ends and doodads. I never could tolerate with functional items not being clearly functional . . . and I certainly didn't want a lot of that junk in my vision, gathering dust, interfering with window-washing, etc. I didn't want any wide trims on the doorways or windows; I wanted it narrow, and use that space . . . to bring me a wider window, give me more light, or give me wider doors.
>
> *Light* has always been somewhat of a specialty of my disposition. I never was happy when I was in—under—an artificial light, rather, in a room if it glared at me. . . . I

did enjoy, early in the morning, to look out and have the sun bright in the foliage around the house that I expected to build, casting some shadows of course, with *curtainless windows*. No bric-a-brac, no funny fixtures on the inside gathering—as I've heretofore said—dust. The walls and the finished trim at the openings . . . for a limited amount of housekeeping and deterioration of finish.

> I wanted to have the bedroom quarters and nursery activities—including a bath, including facilities—separate and exclusively for the use of the children. Naturally, there being expected an oak floor . . . boys and girls . . . the lighting so arranged that the beds were free from shadows or direct light. Also, the window sills had to be a little higher than they would normally be. . . . All this would be offset on the side by a master bedroom with a fireplace and with built-in mirrored cabinets for clothing, instead of the normal kind of devices used for the—

Did he mean dark closets?

> I didn't want any dark closets; I wanted something that was out in the open, where I could see it and where it wouldn't accumulate moths and a lot of junk. . . . The other item of arrangement that I was particularly interested in was to have a child's—or children's—playroom on practically the ground-floor level. The point that I was trying to establish was a safety measure; that the children wouldn't have to run up and down the stairs and slide on the bannisters and all that stuff which was natural with kids.

And the playroom would be next to the court?

> That property or garden—whichever you want to call it—would be the section between the garage and house and a brick retaining wall from the rear and side. These kids could not be gotten out of the yard, nor could they help themselves to foreign travel. They were fully protected; and that should eliminate accidents of serious nature.

Robie was strong-willed, young, cocky and well-to-do; he seems to have had many ideas about his future house. His training in mechanical engineering nevertheless failed to help him translate his wishes into clear visual form:

> The whole thing was so nebulous to form a plan that I could not explain it to anybody. In fact, I pretty well balled-up myself. But my preliminary sketches, such as they were, on scraps of paper . . . I finally transferred to larger sheets with more accuracy, to make them more presentable for outsiders' use—in that I anticipated a limited amount of time to be spent with an architect when I possibly built a house. . . . Finally, I got this shaped-up in such a manner that it was *reasonably* intelligent, and possibly would have looked a little more business-like; and I knew what I wanted, and I wanted to get what I wanted, and to hell with everything else.

---

[8]No written communications between Wright and Robie from the period of 1908–1910 survive in the archives of the Frank Lloyd Wright Foundation, according to Bruce Brooks Pfeiffer, director. Presumably, they mostly dealt face to face or over the telephone.

9. *Susan Lawrence Dana house, 1901–1904, Lawrence Avenue at Fourth Street, Springfield, Ill.*

Well, this worked out all right. These various sketches—these various sheets, we'll call them, in that they . . . numbered half a dozen—were displayed to friends of mine . . . in the building business or the architectural business. These were pretty hard-headed Chicago citizens, who had weathered the storms of politics and many other things in the building of structures. They looked at these things, and they thought I'd gone nuts. Well, maybe so. It was my money, and the limited time that I could spend wouldn't be . . . I believed, illy spent. They said: "No, we're not in that kind of job; we build big stuff. . . ." So they were out. But I did ask their advice and their counsel as to who were the current successful builders of homes. . . .

I had to delay a while . . . because I had a multiplicity of men who'd been accustomed to spending large sums of money, and possibly had expensive ideas. I wanted a house of minimum cost. . . . I did a little traveling about, inspecting some of these products of the then-modern type of home, and ran across a constant thought: "Oh, I know what you want—one of those damn—one of those Wright houses."

Well . . . they pretty well advertised Mr. Wright. And, on contact with him, and seeing some of the work and talking with his ambitions of a different type of buildings—of homes, rather—at that time . . . I became rather interested in his views. And I thought, well, if he was a nut, and I was maybe, we'd get along swell. He agreed that was entirely possible.

Robie didn't say that it was Lora who loved Hyde Park and the university, or that Lora had come from Springfield, where the Susan Lawrence Dana house of 1901–1904 stood close to the center of town, and only two blocks from the governor's mansion, as a splendid sample of Wright's architecture [9]. Fred Robie, jr., speaking of later years, remembered the house well. "In Springfield there is a beautiful Wright house," he said,

"and mother used to teach me—used this house, rather, to teach me—the outstanding features of Mr. Wright's homes of that time."[9] In any event, Robie so thoroughly absorbed Wright's views that when he looked back half a century later his mind wandered from memories of what he had asked for to memories of what Wright designed and memories of the house as he lived in it.

Wright knew how to follow Robie's requests while satisfying his own character as well. The notion of giving Robie a great living room in which he could take command of the street while protecting his own privacy was one that expressed Wright's spirit exactly. America "places a life premium on individuality," Wright wrote in 1910. "This means greater individual life and more privacy in life. . . . It means lives lived in greater independence and seclusion."[10] Only two months before Robie acquired his building site, Wright had published his first "In the Cause of Architecture" essay, detailing the propositions that coincided with what Robie liked to think of as his own program. Wright declared that a building "should contain as few rooms as will meet the conditions

[9]In his March 1908 essay, Wright coyly described the Dana house as "designed to accommodate the art collection of its owner and for entertaining extensively, somewhat elaborately worked out in detail." Mrs. Dana's ambitions took flight rather too soon after the death, on February 17, 1901, of her father, Rheuna D. Lawrence, a former mayor of Springfield. She conspired to withdraw his will, which established trusts for her and her mother, before it was probated and thus she gained early access to his fortune, I was told by Earl R. Bice, an attorney for the family and conservator of Mrs. Dana's estate, in a conversation of September 4, 1964. Mrs. Dana convinced her aging mother that Wright was only going to remodel their Italianate homestead on the large site (160 feet by 241 feet) that Lawrence had bought in 1868. In the end, only the parlor and carriage house survived. She held a housewarming in December 1904. Her mother died in 1905.

[10]Wright, introduction to *Ausgeführte Bauten und Entwürfe von Frank Lloyd Wright* (Berlin, 1910), n.p. Klaus-Jürgen Sembach, in "Five Early Twentieth-Century Villas," *Du*, XXXV (Sept. 1975), pp. 16–19, illustrates the Robie house and perceptively remarks: "Probably no other architect since has been capable of building with so much privacy and intimacy. . . ."

which give it rise and under which we live." He wrote with disdain of houses "cut up into box-like compartments," their spaces "slaughtered with the butt and slash of the old plinth and corner block trim, of dubious origin, and finally smothered with horrible millinery." Too many houses were "mere notion stores, bazaars or junkshops." But he had learned to manage window openings "as elementary constituents of the structure grouped in rhythmical fashion, so that all the light and air and prospect the most rabid client could wish would not be too much from an artistic standpoint." A proper perception of the natural beauty of the Midwestern prairie would lead to houses with "sheltering overhangs, low terraces and out-reaching walls sequestering private gardens."[11] And in a speech as early as 1894, Wright had expressed his distaste for dark closets: "Housewives erroneously gauge convenience by the number and size of dark places in which to pack things out of sight and ventilation . . . as ordinarily used they are breeders of disease and poor housekeeping."[12]

Robie had found his architect; Wright had gained a good client. They had no trouble, Robie recalled, in getting along:

From the first we had a definite community of thought.

. . . When I talked in citizen and mechanical terms, he talked and thought in his architectural terms. We . . . agreed . . . on a final procedure; that he would make sketches and submit them in a reasonable time. I told him flat that, of course, I didn't expect to build immediately—take his time. Which he did do, and how![13]

In the meantime he had not been idle. He spent a great deal of energy and thought and time, and he became more enthusiastic about the possibilities as he was able to work out the puzzle of placing the rooms in relative positions, and so forth. I think it was perhaps five or six months before we agreed on a fixed plan. . . .

At the time of our meeting of minds, so to speak, it was winter. You can't build a house in ten minutes. You have to get contractors, you have to get estimates, you have to get sources of materials—all of which gave us ample time if we waited and started the next year. He was in no hurry, because he had some commitments on hand, and we were not in a hurry.

We were very comfortable, happy . . . and a difference of a few months would mean nothing in our lifetimes. Here was a structure that was going to last as long as we lived, we hoped, and was going to be a comfortable place, and wasn't going to be built-on in corners and whatnot, like the telescopic arrangements of the New England homes of early times.[14]

---

[11]Wright, "In the Cause of Architecture," pp. 156–160.

[12]Frank Lloyd Wright on Architecture, ed. Frederick Gutheim (New York, 1941), p. 3.

[13]Wright never rushed a conception. Pauline Schindler could remember even in 1970 how unhurried he was in 1919 when at work on such large-scale commissions as the Imperial Hotel in Tokyo and the Olive Hill compound for Aline Barnsdall in Los Angeles; see Esther McCoy, Vienna to Los Angeles: Two Journeys (Santa Monica, Calif., 1979), p. 33.

[14]Some 20 years after the house was built, Wright started misdating it to 1906 (see Fig. 34). Robie, too, began to think their meeting of minds had occurred in 1906. Wright often exaggerated the modernity of his designs by a few years, just as he trimmed two years from his age.

Chapter II
CONDITIONS AND CHARACTER

Frank Lloyd Wright looked out across Chicago and found it to be an industrial cinderfield. Barry Byrne of course agreed: in later years, when he spoke of the Oak Park studio as having had a magic about it that savored of a higher order of things, he remembered Chicago as "vast and squalid . . . an inexpressively dreary city, without any delight."[1] Wright assumed the role of a missionary, to help others see as he saw [10]. His sermon, essentially, was simple. Life could be formed anew if new form could be brought to its setting, architecture. In his forty-first year he could already review his own career most poignantly:

> Adler and Sullivan had little time to design residences. The few that were unavoidable fell to my lot. . . . So, largely, it remained for me to carry into the field of domestic architecture the battle they had begun in commercial building. During the early years of my own practice I found this lonesome work. . . . I well remember how "the message" burned within me, how I longed for comradeship until I began to know the younger men.[2]

The first was Robert C. Spencer, jr.:

> Bob and I were often seen together; later he took the office next mine. . . . Chicago conformists working in

10. *Frank Lloyd Wright, the missionary in a cinderfield.*

other offices, seeing us arm in arm down the street, would say in derision, "There goes God-almighty with his Jesus Christ." Bob didn't mind.[3]

Spencer indeed began to serve Wright as a spokesman; he wrote of Wright as a leader of the revolt against dead custom. Wright himself soon asserted that, with the ex-

---

[1]Byrne, in Studs Terkel, *Division Street: America* (New York, 1967), p. 260; also see Wright, *Modern Architecture* (Princeton, N.J., 1931), pp. 5, 42. Forever the optimist, Wright came to think that Chicago someday would be "the most beautiful great city left in the modern world." See *An Organic Architecture*, p. 26.

[2]Wright, "In the Cause of Architecture," p. 156; also see *An Organic Architecture*, pp. 4, 6. Curtis Besinger writes in a letter of January 7, 1974, that "one time at Taliesin Mr. Wright said that as a young man he thought that if he was to accomplish anything in architecture he would need to do it before he was forty years old." John Root had died in 1891 at 41, and H. H. Richardson had died in 1886 at 47.

[3]Wright, *A Testament* (New York, 1957), p. 34. Spencer, who had studied at the Massachusetts Institute of Technology and who was slightly older, began to groom himself like Wright.

ception of the work of Louis Sullivan, his architecture represented the first consistent protest, in bricks and mortar, against the pitiful waste of the times. He had the curious habit of seeing his own art as both radical and conservative, an apparent paradox that nevertheless should never have been hard to resolve. If his values were conservative, his vision most certainly was radical. His work stood for strength, order, discipline, rhythm and that final grace and radiance which arise from right relationships. All was to depend on a new sense of form and especially a new feeling for space as the basic reality of shelter. Space was to be shaped to express freedom, the right of the individual to pursue a richer life.[4]

Almost any of Wright's houses could have told Robie to expect from him something very different. Most of the prominent architects of the day, as Spencer put it, were still busy transplanting exotics. Wright had the force of character to assimilate very quickly anything he liked, and to make it over into something all his own. The work that he offered was as fresh as could be. Just a glimpse of the living-room bay of the B. Harley Bradley

house tells that much [11].[5] Robie must have sensed in Wright's architecture the aura of noble privacy, the power of changing even the most ordinary sites into places of wonder and enchantment.

Wright had been discouraged to discover that so many cultured men and women cared so little for the spiritual integrity of their living environment:

> There are exceptions, and I found them chiefly among American men of business with unspoiled instincts and untainted ideals. A man of this type usually has the faculty of judging for himself. He has rather liked the "idea" and much of the encouragement this work receives comes straight from him because the "common sense" of the thing appeals to him. While the "cultured" are still content with their small châteaux, Colonial wedding cakes, English affectations or French millinery, he prefers a poor thing but his own. He errs on the side of character, at least.[6]

He found in Robie, then, precisely the best kind of client, a venturesome man of business. And he must have been delighted to see Robie's prototype cycle car.[7] Robie lived and worked in a man's world. He never mentioned his wife when he reminisced about the house, and only once referred to "additional gadgets and odds-and-ends" that a "feminine mind" could be expected to drag into a new house, even one so thoroughly designed and furnished. Lora Robie once said her husband told her that when he was away from home and not at work it was none of her business what he was doing. Robie favored his cheerful son, and for the last 50 years of his life managed never to see his daughter. Wright, for his part, was never as convincing when he spoke about the family in American life as he was in talking about the individual. The uncompromising nature of his architecture was hardly intended to accommodate the conflicts in taste that almost invariably occur between husband and wife.

---

[4]See Spencer, "The Work of Frank Lloyd Wright," the *Architectural Review* (Boston), VII (June 1900), p. 72, and Wright, *Ausgeführte Bauten*. In "An Architect's Studio," the *House Beautiful*, VII (Dec. 1899), pp. 44–45, Alfred H. Granger called Wright "a radical opponent of the use of ancient styles." The *Architectural Review*, XV (April 1908), p. 78, described Wright's gospel as a noble "protest." Barry Byrne, writing in *America*, LXIX (June 19, 1943), p. 305, called Wright "probably one of the few consistent Protestants." With such passages as in *The Disappearing City* (New York, 1932), p. 16, where he writes that "individuality is a high attribute of character, seldom common, always radical, and so always truly conservative," Wright encouraged such confusion as is prevalent in Norris Kelly Smith, *Frank Lloyd Wright: A Study in Architectural Content* (Englewood Cliffs, N.J., 1966). A more recent revival of interest in Beaux-Arts design methods has furthered the misinterpretation of Wright as a conservative.

[5]Bradley helped direct a farm-implement business, and his wife was

a sister-in-law of Charles E. Roberts, one of Wright's patrons in Oak Park. There is little reason to believe William Drummond's claim in 1944 that, while Wright was gone one weekend in 1900, Drummond "in one day" designed both the Bradley house and the Warren Hickox house next door; he never showed such genius after leaving Wright. See Suzanne Ganschinietz, "William Drummond," the *Prairie School Review*, VI, No. 1 (1969), p. 7.

[6]Wright, "In the Cause of Architecture," p. 158.

[7]Of all the cars he owned and drove, Wright was most fond of the classic MG "because of its scale," Charles Montooth of the Taliesin Associated Architects reports. This small and personal two-seater, now often replicated, came close in spirit to the open runabout which Robie was trying to manufacture. Robie insisted that his wife learn what made a car work, and she became one of the first women in Chicago to drive. On one of his cars he added a special windshield so that "Sunny" could sit up front. He also gave the boy an elaborate toy car.

What he called a thoroughbred building always implied a commission embodied in one client only.[8]

Radical and masculine, the Robie house would be built in a part of Chicago characteristically stern and urbane. Wright knew Hyde Park and Kenwood from his earliest years in the city.[9] Not surprisingly, the largest house in Kenwood was also the most forbidding [12].[10] Wright's house for Isidor Heller, in Hyde Park, had been only slightly more relaxed [13]. Brick houses faced Woodlawn Avenue from both sides south of Fifty-seventh Street in approaching Robie's site [14]. As a city house, the house for Robie would be compact and protected. It would be built with a generous budget:

OPPOSITE: *11. Detail of the B. Harley Bradley house ("Glenlloyd"), 1900–1901, Harrison Avenue at the Kankakee River, Kankakee, Ill.* ABOVE: *12. Julius Rosenwald house, 1903–1904, at 4901 Ellis Avenue, Chicago. Nimmons & Fellows, architects.* BELOW: *13. Isidor Heller house, 1895–1897, at 5132 Woodlawn Avenue, Chicago.*

[8]Edgar Tafel, in *Apprentice to Genius* (New York, 1979), pp. 64–65, writes that "Mr. Wright's buildings were always the result of a relationship between men, and Mrs. Client was too often in the way. He often said, 'Only fools and women criticize half-done work.' " Among the exceptions were Susan Lawrence Dana, Aline Barnsdall, Mrs. Avery Coonley and Mrs. Edwin Cheney.

[9]"No one will ever call it quaint," Jean F. Block remarks of the Hyde Park–Kenwood area in *Hyde Park Houses* (Chicago, 1978), p. 87. She defines Kenwood as being north of Fifty-first, with Hyde Park Center and South Park lying between Fifty-first and Fifty-ninth. Commuter stations on the Illinois Central lines were built in 1856 at Fifty-third and in 1859 at Forty-seventh. Chicago annexed the entire area in June 1889, the same month that Wright married Catherine Tobin, who lived at Forty-seventh and Kimbark, in Kenwood, and who had attended the Hyde Park High School. Also see Carl Abbott, " 'Necessary Adjuncts to its Growth': The Railroad Suburbs of Chicago, 1854–1875," *Journal of the Illinois State Historical Society*, LXXIII (1980), pp. 117–131.

[10]The site of the Rosenwald house is about 298 feet by 247 feet and the floor area of the main house is about 17,000 square feet. Julius Rosenwald, born and raised in Springfield, Ill., became president of Sears Roebuck in 1909. His philanthropic gifts came to about $63 million.

ABOVE: *14. East side of Woodlawn Avenue, looking south. The houses (from left) at 5707, 5711 and 5715 were all built between 1900 and 1910.* OPPOSITE: *15. The prairie: looking toward the Midway from the south balcony of the Robie house, winter 1913.*

The bank figures and all of their statements I can't lay my hands on right now . . . but in 50 years you get rid of things. They're satisfactory, and you're not so interested in the costs. I was hoping for a happiness . . . a long life and comfortable living for myself and family, of course, and I did not expect this was going to be a house of *too* much criticism or controversy. . . . Now the actual cost of the house proper, including all items—interest, even, and taxes—was $35,000. The cost of the lot was $14,000. The special furnishings . . . approximately $10,000.[11]

That was seven to ten times the budget of a modest house; Wright could pursue the elaboration he instinctively preferred, and thus sustain a distinctive character of design from the outer massing down to the tiniest inner detail.

Wright's ideal was the comprehensive and unified work of art, the *Gesamtkunstwerk*. German culture fascinated him. He spoke of Bach and Beethoven as the two greatest architects, and he confessed his love for the "old Germany" of Goethe, Schiller, even Nietzsche. He liked to trace his grasp of form and space to childhood hours with the kindergarten building elements devised by Friedrich Fröbel. He had discovered in Chicago a community of German-born engineers and architects. During the World's Columbian Exposition a "German vil-

lage" stood only a block south of the site Robie was to buy. Bruno Möhring, a German architect, visited the Oak Park studio in 1904; Kuno Francke, professor of German culture at Harvard, arrived a few years later. Of the 35 professors on the original faculty of the University of Chicago who held doctor's degrees, 14 were from German universities; when Wright left Oak Park in the fall of 1909 and headed for Berlin to prepare the Wasmuth portfolio, he entrusted his downtown office to Hermann Valentin von Holst, whose father was head professor of history at the university and had been hired from the University of Freiburg. Robie was as mechanically inclined as a Bavarian clockmaker. Wright sent him a note as late as 1951 that ended with the salutation "*Gesundheit.*"[12] Discipline, unslackening vigor, power in place of prettiness: those were the German preferences that would inform the house. In later years, Wright often would say that the house became known in Germany as *Dampfer* (steamship) architecture. He was proud that it appealed particularly to the German mind, and pleased with the metaphor of a machine-powered ship.[13]

Wright saw the machine as a thrilling, beneficent instrument for human progress. He discerned in the Arts and Crafts movement a reactionary and sometimes ridiculous spirit; even in 1900 he was eager to nettle C. R. Ashbee, one of its leading voices:

My God . . . is machinery, and the art of the future will be the expression of the individual artist through the thousand powers of the machine, the machine doing all those things that the individual workman cannot do, and the creative artist is the man that controls all this and understands it.[14]

[11]The builder's ledger books are now in the Special Collections at the University of Chicago Library, and show the cost of labor and materials at $26,567.11; the amount of profit is not indicated. Ledgers of the Niedecken-Walbridge Co., now in the Prairie Archives of the Milwaukee Art Museum, show the cost of the furnishings at $6,926.20, including profit. The lot cost $13,500. Wright's fee usually was ten percent of the costs. As an index to the value of the dollar, 52,880 feet of lumber for the house cost only $1,224.51—less than two and a half cents a foot.

[12]The note is dated February 1, 1951, and is among the papers owned by Mrs. O'Connor. See Wright, *An Autobiography* (New York, 1943), *passim*, and *An Organic Architecture*, p. 24. Also see Richard J. Storr, *Harper's University* (Chicago, 1966), pp. 75–76, and Thomas Wakefield Goodspeed, *A History of the University of Chicago* (Chicago, 1916).

[13]Wright thought it his duty to idealize the client's character and tastes, so the client would feel "he would rather have his house than any other he has ever seen." See "In the Cause of Architecture," p. 162. For the *Dampfer* allusion, see *An Autobiography*, p. 252; *A Testament*, p. 76; and *Sixty Years of Living Architecture: Frank Lloyd Wright* (Los Angeles, 1954), n.p. One of Wright's first mature designs, significantly, was inspired by a commission from the Yahara Boat Club at the University of Wisconsin: a small, streamlined shelter for rowing shells.

[14]Recorded by Ashbee in his journals after he met Wright late in 1900; see Alan Crawford, "Ten letters from Frank Lloyd Wright to Charles Robert Ashbee," *Architectural History*, 13 (1970), p. 64. Crawford reports that the black keys on Ashbee's piano were replaced by purple ones. Such artiness hardly was akin to Wright's virile style. In the column capitals by the entrance to his Oak Park studio of 1898, Wright had Richard Bock sculpture scrawny secretary birds: "a quiet fling at the reactionary spirits who dominate the 'Arts and Crafts' movement," Spencer noted in 1900.

Ashbee spoke of fighting the battle of the hand against the machine, so that good men and women could reclaim the joys of labor. Wright sneered at the idea of amateurs pounding their fingers in making useless things; not for him the innocent charm or nursery-like naïveté of these latter-day Medievalists. He turned instead to the swift, sure lines and clean planes that could express the machine. Of course the Robie house would be built of many parts, not merely extruded from a machine. Yet its parts would be machine-formed, not hand-carved. The kind of beauty needed to build human character, Wright wrote, should be as organic a revelation of modern conditions as a dynamo or battleship.[15]

A building site so close to the University of Chicago was bound to stir in Wright a special response. Never had the progressive, zealous spirit of the university found visual expression. Nothing about the campus suggested that the academic community made any connection between the life of the mind and the creation of an appropriately modern environment. To the contrary; the buildings were conceived as nostalgic evocations of Cambridge and Oxford. Wright rebelled at such sentimentality:

> Our Chicago University, "a seat of learning," is just as far removed from the truth [as steel-frame skyscrapers dressed in stone to recall historical styles]. If environment is significant and indicative, what does this highly reactionary, extensive and expensive scene-painting by means of hybrid Collegiate Gothic signify? . . . why should an American University in a land of Democratic ideals in a Machine Age be characterized by secondhand adaptation of Gothic forms . . .?[16]

Wright called instead for a revival of the Gothic spirit, a

search for simple conventions to make peace with nature and to interpret the ideals of modern life. He had absorbed the lectures of Viollet-le-Duc.[17] Gothic principles could work together very well in the fabric of the Robie house, its plan beautifully articulated by independent yet harmonious points of support, the court walled as if a cloister, and the entrance passage planned to lead from darkness at the west door to a long vessel of light above.

Then came the prominence of the site, at the very edge of residential Hyde Park. The vista to the south skimmed over the undeveloped block from Fifty-eighth Street to Fifty-ninth Street, then clear across the Midway Plaisance, reaching almost 1,400 feet to a row of apartment buildings at Sixtieth Street [15]. The land was flat (except for slight depressions in the open block and at the center of the Midway) and to jaded eyes the

---

[15]See his 1900 speech to the Architectural League, in *Frank Lloyd Wright on Architecture*, p. 6; his Hull-House speech of 1901, in *Modern Architecture*, p. 8; his words on the Larkin Building, in "In the Cause of Architecture," p. 167, and his speech to Chicago businessmen, in the *Western Architect*, XXIV (Sept. 1916), p. 122. H. P. Berlage, the Dutch architect, toured Wright's work during a visit to America in 1911 and wrote later that it was a "charming and lovable art, at the root of which the mechanical lies only apparently"; see *The Life-Work of the American Architect Frank Lloyd Wright* (Santpoort, Holland, 1925–1926; new edition, New York, 1965), p. 82. William L. MacDonald, in his *Piranesi's Carceri: Sources of Invention* (Northampton, Mass., 1979), p. 27, accurately remarks the machinery-like plan of the Johnson Wax Company Building of 1936–1939 (a metaphor that suggests the smoothing of life's chores).

[16]Wright, *Modern Architecture*, pp. 9–10. The university was founded by John D. Rockefeller, a devout Baptist (at least in his own mind), and organized by William Rainey Harper, a Baptist and brilliant scholar of Hebrew. Classes began October 1, 1892. From the first, the university stood as a bastion of free inquiry and Christian reform. It claimed the first sociology department and the first academically supported settlement house. Wright nevertheless said that sev-

eral "brilliant disciples of Ruskin and Morris" at the university had kept the Chicago Arts and Crafts Society reactionary. Mrs. Avery Coonley studied with John Dewey, who was named head of the philosophy department in 1894 and, soon afterward, head of the pedagogy department (later the school of education), a notably progressive part of the university. Mrs. Edwin Cheney, who became Wright's companion, studied with the novelist Robert Herrick. Wright in 1909–1910 planned a summer colony in Montana for a group of the university's professors. He wrote of Dr. Ferdinand Schevill, professor of modern history, as his best friend. He was so impressed by Thorstein Veblen, one of the original fellows of the faculty and a perceptive critic of "the higher learning," that he listed him among the sources of his *Autobiography*. Veblen, too, was a native of Wisconsin (as was Gustav Stickley, the reformist furniture-maker, who, much like Wright, said that his early days on the farm had led him to simplicity and the habit of going at things in a natural way). Eight houses in Robie's block had been built for professors. The fact that Wright spent less than a year as a university student in Wisconsin must have intensified his desire to compete with the academic environment.

[17]See my essay on "Frank Lloyd Wright and Viollet-le-Duc," *JSAH*, XXVIII (Oct. 1969), pp. 173–183.

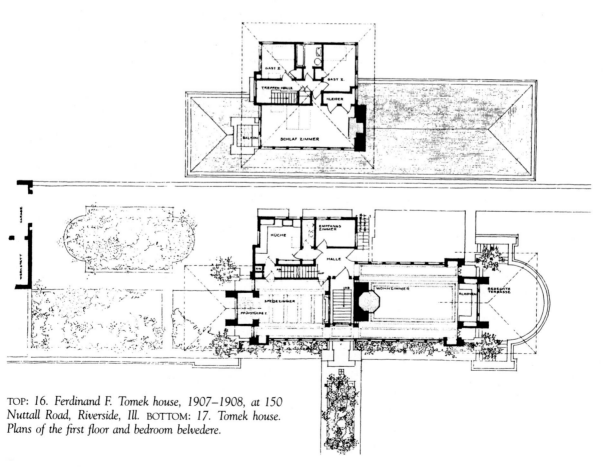

TOP: 16. Ferdinand F. Tomek house, 1907–1908, at 150
Nuttall Road, Riverside, Ill. BOTTOM: 17. Tomek house.
Plans of the first floor and bedroom belvedere.

prospect lacked any interest. Wright stood almost alone in his intuition of the prairie:

> We of the Middle West are living on the prairie. The prairie has a beauty of its own and we should recognize and accentuate this natural beauty, its quiet level. Hence, gently sloping roofs, low proportions, quiet sky lines, suppressed heavy-set chimneys and sheltering overhangs, low terraces and out-reaching walls sequestering private gardens.[18]

Everything about the site suggested a long, low, streamlined, shiplike house: the prairie, the nearby lake, the new sense of speed, the still unshaken faith in the machine, and the shape of the lot, three times as long as it was wide.[19]

Three other facts distinguished the site: it was at the corner; the houses to the north were elevated by an embankment two feet higher than the sidewalk; and by covenant every house was set back 35 feet from the west lot line. To take advantage of the corner, Wright would turn the house two ways. The entrance and the street address could respect Woodlawn Avenue while the broad reach of the house favored the south, so as not to sacrifice daylight, the breezes of summer, the low sun of winter or the long view across the Midway.[20] By eliminating the embankment, Wright could lower the house at the same time as he shifted the main rooms a story above. In place of the earth terrace he would create a series of horizontal planes: a long south balcony and concrete platform below it, a west porch, a northwest balcony over a paved entrance court, and small balconies off the dining room and the master bedroom. As to the setback covenant, Wright would slyly follow the letter while violating its spirit; what he called the porch would be in fact an integral part of the house, serving the living room as a balcony.[21]

Finally, there was the precedent of his house for Ferdinand F. Tomek on four adjacent lots which overlooked the Long Common in Riverside, Illinois [16, 17]. He described the Tomek house as intended for the low and damp prairie, thus designed with a basement entirely above ground, an entrance leading directly upstairs to the main living spaces, and bedrooms assigned to a small upper story. Barry Byrne remembered being in charge of the working drawings for the Tomek house and supervising its construction:

> This . . . house is a less developed, and accordingly less successful, use of the same general plan and building mass as the Robie House. It was characteristic of Mr. Wright's procedure that he would work on an architectural idea until he felt he had brought it to relative completeness. Often this development occurred during the preparation of the working drawings, and erasing and redoing the working drawings . . . was a usual and often wearisome procedure. To me the reward was to see emerge from Wright's hand designs so clarified and unified . . . that the amazing result is as clear to me today as it was evident to me when the transformation occurred under my youthful eye. . . . Failing adequate development in his initial use of a given scheme he would sometimes do as he did in the Robie House, repeat the architectural scheme of another house, in this case the one built for Mr. Tomek, but with the new design highly developed. . . . The emergence of Wright as an architect in that great period of his development, when it was my good fortune to work under him, also saw the recession of Wright as a draftsman . . . he transformed himself from the more superficial precision of the draftsman type into a master architect whose occupation was no longer mere delineation, but whose concern was that immeasurably greater thing, the large-scale manipulation of spaces and masses into a vital, intrinsic architecture . . . by 1908, when I left the studio, by sheer force of circumstances Wright as draftsman had almost ceased to exist and that more vital being, Wright as architect, was operating in full possession of his extraordinary creative power.[22]

---

[18]Wright, "In the Cause of Architecture," p. 157. It was intended that the Midway serve as a drainage system and waterway between Washington Park and Jackson Park. Olmsted, Vaux & Co. in 1871 had planned 14 acres of basins bordered by pleasure walks, but the Midway remained only a sweep of grass. Frederick Law Olmsted saw in the environs of Chicago nothing but a flat and mostly treeless terrain, "not merely uninteresting, but, during much of the year, positively dreary." His condescension was put to shame by Wright's profound response to the prairie.

[19]A survey dated March 18, 1909, now in the Special Collections of the University of Chicago Library, shows the lot to be 60 feet by 180 feet five-eighths inches.

[20]Wright wrote of "light, air and prospect, the enjoyable things one goes to the suburbs to secure," in "A Small House with 'Lots of Room in It,' " the *Ladies Home Journal*, XVIII (July 1901), p. 15. His house for Isidor Heller, at 5132 Woodlawn, was also addressed to the south.

[21]The instrument, dated April 9, 1895, is defined by Moses W. Gray, one of the subdividers, as a covenant "for the purpose of creating and perpetuating a uniform building line." It is filed in the Cook County Recorder's microfiche library as reg. doc. 2212632. A point 35 feet east of the lot line would come close to the center of the salient post in the living-room prow; the west wall of the porch is only 18 feet four inches from the lot line.

[22]Byrne, rev. of *The Drawings of Frank Lloyd Wright*, p. 109. In *Ausgeführte Bauten*, Wright described the Tomek house as a suburban residence and characteristic prairie house, adding that the plan "was later elaborated into the plan of the Robie house." Tomek, whose business was listed as room moldings, bought the site in 1905, writes Maya Moran, who now lives in the house. Drawings for the house were exhibited in the 1907 annual of the Chicago Architectural Club. The account books of the Niedecken-Walbridge Co. of Milwaukee show that Tomek was still buying furniture for his house in the spring of 1909.

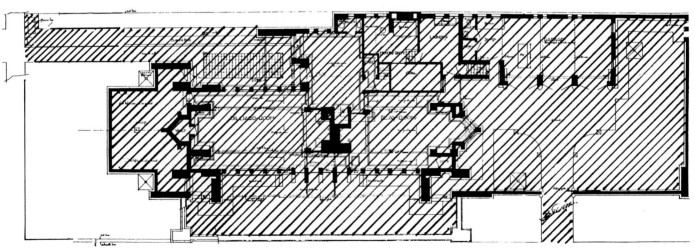

TOP: *18. South front of the Robie house.* BOTTOM: *19. The house in relation to its building site.* OPPOSITE: *20. Plan of bedroom story and roofs.*

Chapter III
PLANS AND CONSTRUCTION

Wright did take his time. He was busy during 1908 with more than a dozen commissions, and he needed time to nurture the plan of the Robie house far beyond that of the Tomek house. In the end, the differences would be more important than the similarities. Somehow, the site of the Tomek house seemed not greatly affected by his architecture; the house deferred to the trees and lawn, and its rhythm was almost rural. The walls were plain and stuccoed, the entrances easy of access, the plan relatively simple and so too the patterns in the glass. Friendly and unguarded, the Tomek house essentially was at ease. By contrast, the Robie house was going to glide across the ground to leave only a vestige of that sea of grass which typically surrounds a residence in the Middle West [18, 19].

In relation to what Robie had in mind, his building site was small. The house could hardly commune with the prairie if its rooms were stacked high, as in a more traditional town house.[1] Wright knew very well that when space was precious architecture could become all the more vital. With an acute relation of house to site, the plan would gain an intrinsic drama. The plan form is well revealed by a drawing of the bedroom story with the roofs below it: two parallel and adjacent vessels appear to be slipping past each other [20]. Each, like the site, is a long rectangle. Each measures about half the length of the site. The vessels lie against each other, like two bricks. The main vessel, intended for the family, advances toward the salient corner to command the streets and catch sunlight even in the late autumn or winter

---

[1]From the foundation plan it is clear that the court walls and the north side of the house are contiguous with the lot lines. The south garden wall steals four inches past the lot line, and the terminals extend four inches farther. In a deviation typical of Wright's distaste for routine symmetries, the axis of the main vessel does not fall at the center of the lot; it is 28 feet three inches from the south lot line and 31 feet nine inches from the north.

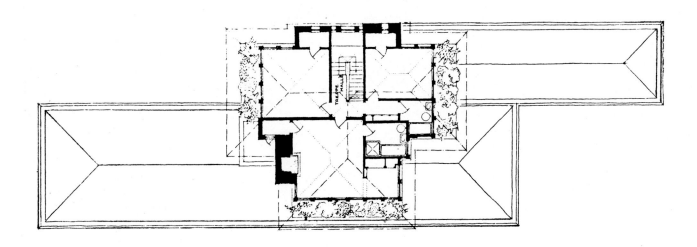

20   Frank Lloyd Wright's Robie House

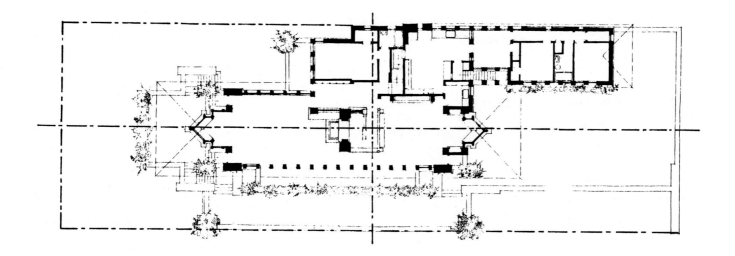

OPPOSITE, TOP: *21. South front.* OPPOSITE, BOTTOM: *22. South front, court wall and service vessel.* ABOVE: *23. Site plan divided into quadrants.* BELOW: *24. Foundation plan, dated March 23, 1909, and signed by Robie.*

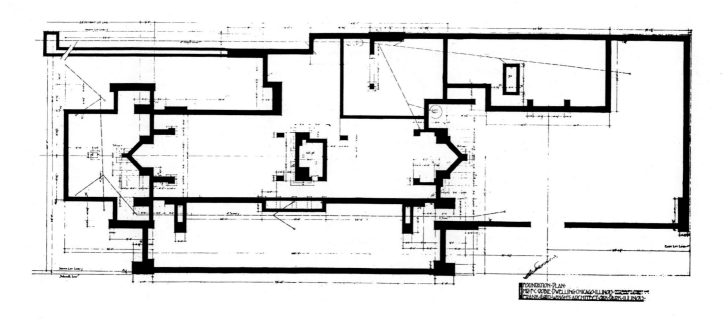

[21]. The lesser vessel, mostly for service, retreats behind a tall court wall to stretch across the back of the site [22].[2]

Wright departs from his usual cruciform and pinwheel plans, and gives to the plan of the Robie house a rare beauty and dynamism generated by a new kind of asymmetric balance. He sees the contradiction of a central chimney mass taking the place of a central crossing. Mass, after all, blocks space; so he assigns the chimney mass almost entirely to the living room. Where is the center of the house? At the top of the stairs to the great vessel [23]. Wright reaches his goal, the "tranquil emphasis on space as the reality of the building."[3]

By the end of March 1909, the working drawings are at hand and Robie has signed them [24–33]:

At this time we both—Mr. Wright and myself—were

[2]The lack of a minor vessel made the Tomek house end abruptly and off-balance. The garage and shop were separated from the house, and the maid's room was on the ground floor near the furnace and laundry rooms.

[3]Wright, *A Testament* (New York, 1957), p. 86.

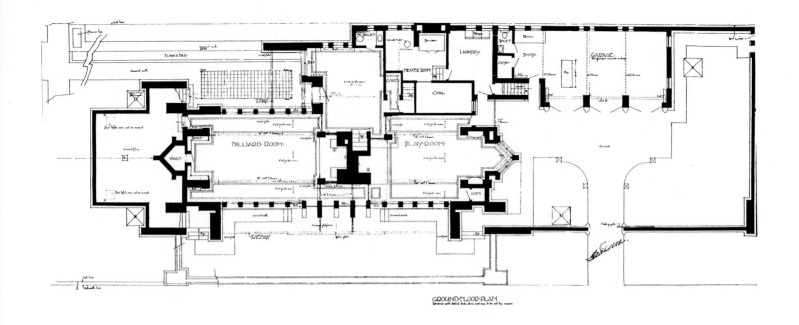

GROUND·FLOOR·PLAN·

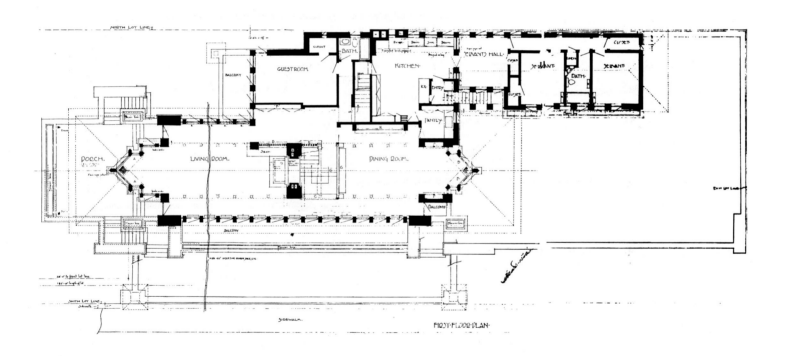

FIRST·FLOOR·PLAN·

TOP: 25. *Ground-floor plan.* BOTTOM: 26. *First-floor plan. The proportions are not right, because the draftsman has omitted one bay from the living room; he notes: "Add 4'0" inserting window, pier, etc." Doors to the south balcony were changed later to paired French doors, and the end bays were changed to windows over light wells.*

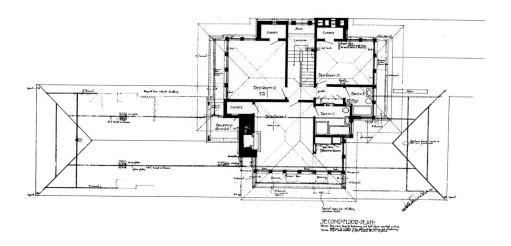

JECOND·FLOOR·PLAN·

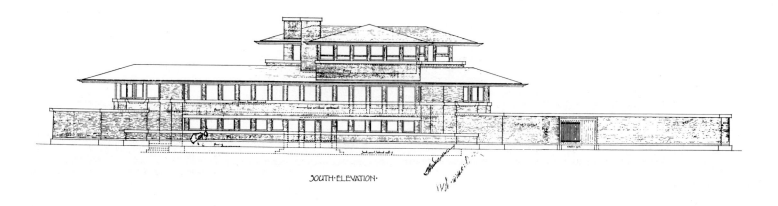

JOUTH·ELEVATION·

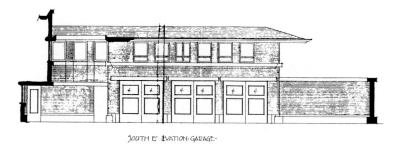

JOUTH·ELEVATION·GARAGE·

TOP: 27. Second-floor plan. Dotted lines in bedrooms and hall show slanted ceilings. Lines on main roof indicate steel cantilever beams. MIDDLE: 28. South elevation of the main vessel. The draftsman errs again, showing only three doors to the south garden. The gates to the garage court were later elaborated. BOTTOM: 29. South elevation of the service vessel. The door at far left leads to the laundry and furnace rooms; the passage near the first garage port leads to a concealed stairway to the kitchen entry.

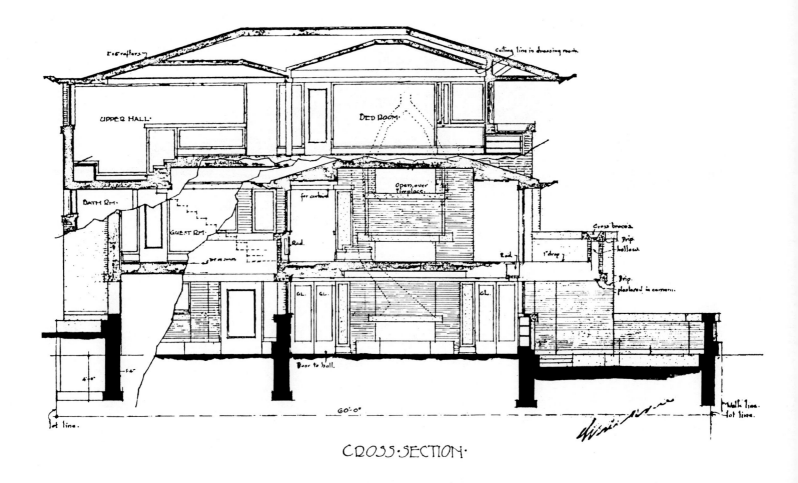

CROSS·SECTION·

OPPOSITE, TOP: 30. *West elevation. The draftsman had labeled this the east elevation.* OPPOSITE, MIDDLE: 31. *North elevation. The house sinks below the terrace of its neighbors.* OPPOSITE, BOTTOM: 32. *East elevation. The draftsman called this the west elevation.* ABOVE: 33. *Section, looking east. The house creeps past the south lot line.*

highly in accord on every line to the last inch. And we agreed that there should be no deviation whatsoever from these specifications . . . without consultation, in which we would include the contractor, of course. This worked out ideally. I had business trips to take elsewhere that carried me away from a week to four weeks at a time; and during the interval I felt it was in perfect hands. And I think it was probably one of the smartest things I ever did, because I wasn't worrying about details. All that I wanted was a house. . . . Ultimately, it worked out to be one of

the cleanest business deals I ever had. . . . His enthusiasm matched my own as we saw things growing in a formally, highly mental attitude of hopefulness . . . a little bit skeptical in some things, because of the criticism of a—advice of many people, and the conversations with a few people who had seen these sketches . . . a perspective view of the house as it probably would turn out . . . other than color, of course. No details of design of windows. . . .

Robie must have been remembering the elevation drawings, which show no panes or patterns in the windows or doors; some of the drawings for glass designs are dated as late as November 1909. No perspective studies have survived from 1909, and probably none was ever made. A starkly abstract rendering often mistaken as a presentation drawing was made twenty years after the plans by an apprentice named Heinrich Klumb, later known as

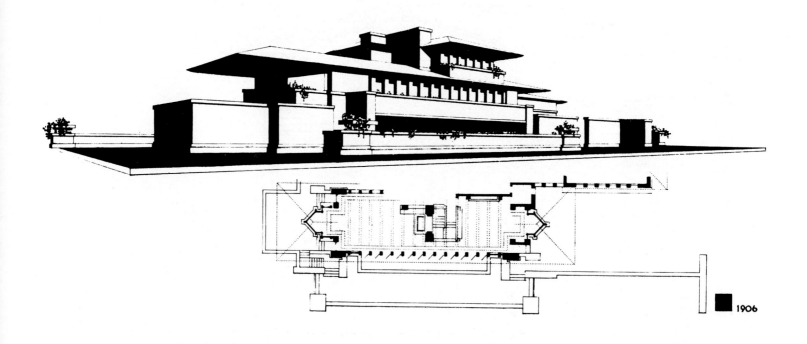

TOP: *34. Rendering, 1929. The date on it errs by three years; the plan also misrepresents the light wells and the doors to the south balcony, and shows no way into the court.* BOTTOM: *35. Rendering, 1910. One bay is missing from the living room.* OPPOSITE: *36. Harrison B. Barnard, the builder.*

Henry Klumb [34].[4] With his training as a mechanical engineer, Robie must have been able to understand the plans without the crutch of a pretty perspective; and Wright thought little of perspectives except when they served to convince a client to build. Barry Byrne recalled that perspectives, if any, typically came last:

> Although Mr. Wright is sometimes pictured as studying his compositions in perspective, this was not his way when I worked under him. The designs he made existed primarily in those greatest of his contributions to a living architecture, his incomparable building plans. The value of his exterior massing and details derived from their appearance of inevitability and from the fact of their indisputable rightness as expressions of the plan. Endowed as he was with an unerring sense of the third dimension, Mr. Wright . . . always arrived at his designs in plan and elevation.[5]

In the picture of the house drawn in Europe for Wright's portfolio of 1910 the point of vantage is imaginary [35]. Although the great length of the main vessel is poorly represented by the foreshortening and the error of omitting one bay from the living room, the sight of the *Dampfer* in harbor is nonetheless thrilling. Space becomes art, and nature is invited aboard; flowers and vines spill from the parapets.

After accepting the plans, Robie's next step is to get the house in construction:

> So . . . we decided that we'd go ahead, build the house, find out whether these bids and so on were actual bids of the exact cost to us, whether they had gone up, or, fortunately to us, perhaps had gone down. As a matter of fact, bids were *reduced*, because of the nature of the knowledge given the contractor, and the specifications had been studied by the suppliers and they found sources of cutting corners and giving us benefits. It was a most happy solution. . . . Mr. Wright had done a beautiful job

of weeding out the contractors and whatnot, and that of course was somewhat evidenced by the bids they put in— all the little details, which he covered with meticulous care. I was amazed.

Robie told his son that the builder was "a go-gettin', two-fisted, high-spittin' sort of guy" who had started in the business at 16 by carrying beer to the laborers on hot days. But he was thinking of the wrong man, perhaps a foreman. Harrison Bernard Barnard, who was born in 1872 in Seville, Ohio, had attended the College of Wooster for two years before he moved to Chicago and enrolled in the new university just as Cobb Hall, its first classroom building, was being finished. He graduated in 1895 and he joined his father, W. E. Barnard, as a builder. He also taught mathematics at Grand Crossing High School and, for his own enjoyment, continued to pursue Latin and Greek. He is remembered even today as a reticent and studious man [36].[6]

Barnard built the house from the spring of 1909 until the spring of 1910; furnishings continued to be added into the fall of 1910. He kept snapshots showing the stages of construction. Others, taken by Robie and by his

---

[4]Klumb had come from Germany aware that the younger architects and critics there were opposed to Wright's work. In a letter of September 5, 1980, he recounts the origin of the abstract rendering: "Assembled and sitting with F.Ll.W. around a fire in the studio one winter day in 1929, discussing this and other matters of 'Organic Architecture,' I suggested that we might try to reduce his delicate renderings of his best-known buildings to a two-dimensional black-on-white graphic presentation 'Modern Architects' were addicted to. His answer: 'Do it.' [Takehiko] Okami and I went to work and produced several, including in addition to the Robie House (drawn by myself) the Winslow House, Yahara Boat Club, Bock Atelier, Unity Temple, and the Larkin Building. All were drawn in ink on roll-up window shades . . . even the stark graphic black-on-white surface presentations did not produce a two-dimensional effect, rather emphasized the depth of his poetry and the power of the third dimension. Nothing 'International Architecture' had to show could equal it."

[5]Byrne, "On Frank Lloyd Wright and His Atelier," *AIA Journal*, 39 (June 1963), p. 110.

[6]Barnard became a trustee of the University of Chicago in 1927. In 1942, when he turned 70, he was named a life trustee. He also served as a trustee of the Shedd Aquarium and, in 1927–1928, as the president of the Union League Club.

chauffeur, named Brady, also survive.[7] The first view in Barnard's series shows the foundations. Two men are at work while a third (apparently Wright, wearing long hair, a floppy cap and a rubberized coat) stands resolutely on a foundation wall and faces east toward the lake, as though captain of the *Dampfer* [37].[8]

Robie remembered the foundation work:

The construction that Mr. Wright had planned was such that we didn't have to have a great lot of deep foundations, because of the sand on the land adjacent to the lake: that area was entirely sand, for probably three or four feet deep.

There was practically no delay in attempting to put in the chimney structure, which was going to be kind of a central supporting member of the house, and the sidewalls went up carefully. Every two or three layers of brick, in order to preserve the continuity and long-line appearance, was checked by the contractor, Mr. Barnard . . . by instruments. There wasn't any guess-or-by-God business, and no chalk lines were satisfactory to him.

He did a beautiful job. It was a piece of art work, it was

TOP: 37. *Foundations, April–May 1909. Looking northwest; Goodman house at upper right. The man staring eastward appears to be Wright.* BOTTOM: 38. *Fred Robie, jr., at the site, May 1909.*

a piece of skill, and it developed into what I wanted and what was satisfactory to Mr. Wright from the standpoint of design and appearance. He was responsible for that, and he took his responsibility very seriously. I know that he frequently was on the job bright and early in the morning, and stayed as long as Mr. Barnard could settle things promptly and satisfactorily.

By the middle of May 1909 the brick walls stand high, especially in the world of "Sunny" [38]. But the masons have made a mistake; at the doors from the billiard room

---

[7]The 30 sequential but undated construction snapshots are owned by W. B. Barnard. Lorraine Robie O'Connor has the family pictures, most of which can be dated because of her mother's habit of noting the exact ages of the children (Lorraine Robie was born December 2, 1909).

[8]The view can be dated to late April or early May 1909 because the first payment ($28.35) to Arthur Meagher, the masonry subcontractor, was made on April 27 and the second ($2,500) on May 24. Fred Robie, jr., said his father told him that all materials were delivered on horse-drawn wagons.

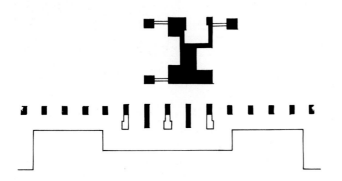

to the garden they have built five full piers [39].[9] Only the second and fourth were planned as piers to carry the transverse steel beams in support of the south balcony; the others, like bollards, were to bring rhythm to the space and to express the orientation of the house to the south [40]. As the workers started over, Wright refined the stone copings by widening the terminals much the same as he shaped interior stair posts [41]. All is in order by the middle of June, when "Sunny" is back at play [42]. Such photographs stirred his memory half a century later:

> Now my own childhood recollections of the house are few but rather vivid. I remember enjoying visits to the job . . . having fun in the huge sandpile used in making mortar and concrete—to the confusion of the workmen perhaps—and walking on the board catwalks that were used to wheelbarrow materials to the house. Those were the high bridges of my earliest memories. In some cases, the boards were at least a foot high off the ground.

Wright understood so well the materials of his art that he could combine them into a structure that would look

TOP, LEFT: 39. *Incorrectly built piers (center) at doors to garden, May–June 1909.* MIDDLE: 40. *Piers as rebuilt.* BOTTOM: 41. *Plan diagram of the piers as rebuilt. The face of the middle capstone is the same width as the capstones of the living-room prow.* TOP, RIGHT: 42. *"Sunny" Robie back at play, June 1909.*

[9]A penciled order to "Take down & rebuild" appears on the builder's set of blueprints, now in the Special Collections at the University of Chicago Library. Contractors often complained of Wright's sketchy working drawings, just as Barry Byrne complained of the preliminary drawings: "Even I, who developed the designs . . . into working drawings, and supervised their construction, in my student days with him, found the plans hard to decipher." See his review of *In the Nature of Materials*, in *Liturgical Arts*, XI (Feb. 1943), p. 49.

ABOVE: *43. Looking northeast, summer 1909.* BELOW: *44. Looking northwest, autumn 1909.* OPPOSITE: *45. Looking northeast, autumn 1909.*

all-of-a-piece and yet reveal each, on close inspection, in its essential character.[10] Robie watched his house rise with walls of brick, copings and sills of cut stone, floors and balconies of reinforced concrete, beams of steel and a final story framed of wood [43].[11]

Inside, work continued through the fall and winter [44, 45].[12] Robie was pleased:

It wasn't long before we were under cover. I went away

and came back and found a roof on and the side walls up, and they were getting ready to cover the concrete floors with wood trim—and a beautiful job they did of that. That, of course, was a beautiful time . . . you could get wood that is pretty difficult today. It was outstandingly cross-grained in some places, just enough to make it most attractive and yet not tiresome to the eye.

Well, these details included of course . . . the building of indirect lighting around the side walls of the living

[10]Louis H. Sullivan at the end of his life wrote quite beautifully that Wright was gifted with "an apprehension of the material, so delicate as to border on the mystic, and yet remain coordinate with those facts we call real life." See his "Reflections on the Tokyo Disaster," the *Architectural Record*, 55 (Feb. 1924), p. 116.

[11]Fred Robie, jr., was totally in error when he said that the structure used 15-inch welded steel girders 100 to 110 feet long, shop-fabricated by the Ryerson Steel Co. The main roof cantilevers in fact rely on 12-inch channel beams; the connections, visible through ceiling traps and light grilles, are bolted; the steel is stamped "Lackawanna," and the revised shop drawings and specifications from the South Halsted St. Iron Works, dated May 6, 1909, show the longest girder at 60 feet

and a variety of sections composed of channels, angles and H-shapes. Barnard began paying the Iron Works on April 29, and the largest payment ($756.95) was on May 27, 1909. Other suppliers and sub-contractors included Thomlinson & Riley (stone); the Wm. Balhatchet Co. (plastering); Chicago Sash, Door & Blind (millwork); Purdy & Cauble (cornices); the Rittenhouse & Embree Lumber Co.; and the Orr & Lockett Hardware Co.

[12]Ledgers of the Barnard Co. note that roughing was finished August 21, 1909; the house was ready for the lathers September 22; electricians were still at work October 5; and trimming began October 26. Payments for millwork, plastering and roofwork continued into the summer of 1910.

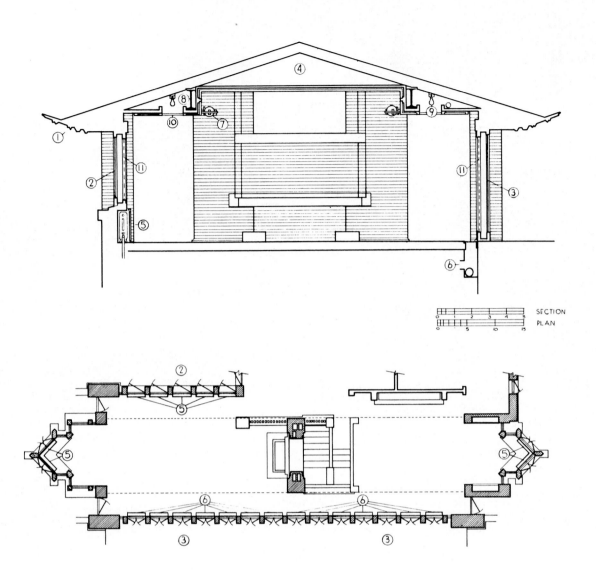

SECTION
PLAN

room. It meant new methods of introducing indirect heating, by having the radiators strung along in front of the doorways and windows, in some cases with the pipes below, actually. . . . These passages and so on aided greatly in having the floors warm, and there was no shock of stepping on a cold floor, particularly in the bedrooms. It was very interesting, and was carried out in very great detail . . . [46].

I was satisfied with the job . . . and every single detail had worked out . . . as we had anticipated and hoped. Relationships with Mr. Wright were ideal. Professional, sure; I didn't have to kiss him for getting a good job done, and what he wanted was a check—I assumed. He never asked me for money.

It seems inconceivable that the foresight, the knowledge and the intense desire to do just the right thing could have been imbedded in a man like him. Possibly it was in his hair. Remember? It was kind of long.

Wright left Oak Park for Europe in late September 1909, to be gone for more than a year. He assigned an assistant to follow the finishing of the house; the furnishings could proceed at a relaxed and careful pace under the control of the Niedecken-Walbridge Co. of Milwaukee. George M. Niedecken, born in Milwaukee in 1878, was a master interior architect who had studied in Berlin and Paris from 1899 to 1902, and who had painted the sumac murals of the Dana house in 1904. He had the grace to submerge his own taste when called upon to serve Wright. In the fall of 1909 he was still at work furnishing the Tomek and Coonley houses in Riverside, as well as the Meyer May house in Grand Rapids, Michigan, a smaller but intricately detailed residence. He first visited Robie's house in the second week of September, just before Wright left, and from October

OPPOSITE: *46. First-floor section and plan diagrams of lighting, heating and cooling: (1) deep eaves for sun control; (2–3) windows and doors for ventilation; (4) mechanical hot-air extraction through upper spaces and duct in chimney; (5–6) concealed radiators; (7–10) lights at soffits, concealing main cantilever beams; (11) storm sash or screens.* LEFT, TOP: *47. Looking northeast, winter 1909–1910.* LEFT, BOTTOM: *48. South front, winter 1909–1910.* BELOW: *49. South front, early 1910.*

1909 until May 1910 he made at least eight more trips there.[13]

Two winter views of the unfinished house show small evergreens in the flower boxes, hardly what Wright would have had in mind [47, 48]. Barnard's last construction photograph, taken from the open field to the south, captures the entire reach of the house and proves his accurate perception of its orientation and character [49]. By now, the great stone flower urns are in place, framing

---

[13]As recorded in the Niedecken-Walbridge Co. ledgers. Niedecken was taught German as a child, and as a professional he subscribed to *Die Kunst*. He saw Robie twice in October to discuss the drawings and color work, returned November 3 to measure the house for rugs, December 14–15 to "superintend color work," December 30 to select embroidery yarns for the spreads, March 25–26, 1910 (unspecified purpose), April 15 to fasten down the rugs, and again on May 20.

ABOVE: *50. Lora Robie with Lorraine and "Sunny," May 1910.*
RIGHT: *51. "Sunny" at home, May 1910.*

the south garden wall. Most of the furniture had been made by the end of February, the eight pairs of portieres (doorway curtains) were ready in March, the larger rugs in April; Robie was to make his largest payment to the Niedecken-Walbridge Co. in May 1910, the same month he photographed Lora and the children at home on Woodlawn Avenue [50, 51]:

> It developed that Mr. Barnard's estimates on labor were a bit out of line, but it was more than compensated by the slight differences in the costs of materials. When the figure was submitted and the checks passed to Mr. Barnard, I was grateful beyond all imagination, because by that time I had been partially moved into this home and had thoroughly inspected it, and was happy with every single detail. There was a guy I felt like kissin'.[14]
>
> A summation of this whole transaction—except my moving expense, the license fees, the telephone fees, and whatnot—came less than we had originally expected . . .

---

[14]Barnard was not so happy, and he never again worked with Wright. He told his son that there were difficulties in payments. A close attention to costs resulted in savings, which in turn allowed an upgrading of materials. Stone sills were added to all the north windows, the north retaining wall by the flower bed was built of stone instead of concrete, so were the leading steps to the west porch and from the south garden, and the cornice was made of copper in place of galvanized iron. Two radiators were added at the west end of the billiard room.

worked out ideally, and *under* the figure that Mr. Wright and I had agreed was reasonable.

Were there any major extras? his son asked.

> Cryin' out loud, no! I would have been able to buy the best dinner in the world for Mr. Wright, Mr. Barnard and a few good friends, and if you had been old enough it would have been fine for you to have been there, too.

And the original budget?

> $60,000. Nobody knew, except my father, how much money I was going to spend for a house, and he didn't think I was such a damn fool as that.

No major changes in the plans?

> I doubt very much if there was a single extra screw or piece of hardware necessary; it was perfectly wonderful. . . . The detailed arrangement was so perfect that Barnard afterwards told me that he might as well have been making a piece of *machinery*. . . . I don't know about that, but it was satisfactory and the house is still up, and I think in pretty good condition the last time I saw it. And that's half a century. I wish I'd stood up as well for the last 50 years.

Chapter IV
FROM THE OUTSIDE IN

When it was finished and in fresh flower, the Robie house stood as something new under the sun, saying exactly what Wright wanted it to say: every man in America had the peculiar and inalienable right to live in his own house in his own way [52]. "He is a pioneer in every right sense of the word," Wright wrote of the American homeowner. "His home environment may face forward, may portray his character, tastes and ideas, if he has any, and every man here has some somewhere about him."[1] Elsewhere in the portfolio of 1910, Wright described the Robie house in a long caption:

A city dwelling with a south front, built of slender brown bricks, with stone trimmings. Roofs tiled, with copper cornices.

A single room type, similar to Tomek, Coonley and Thomas houses, well open to the south, with balcony and enclosed garden. Sleeping-rooms added in belvedere. Garage connected to house, with servants-rooms over. No excavation except for heater and coal.

A highly developed working out of organic relation between exterior and interior—clean, sweeping lines and low proportions preserving openness and airiness of feature and arrangement throughout.

He left undescribed all those nuances which gave the house its strength, all those shifts to and fro in the mysterious realm of outer and inner space. Eric Mendelsohn toured Chicago with Barry Byrne and found in the best of Wright's work an architectural imagination of unheard-of richness. "It is the ecstasy of power in ordering space: a dazzling shower of sparks," Mendelsohn wrote to his wife in Germany. "No one else approaches him."[2]

Surely no one else would have embraced so many opposite tendencies to resolve them so well. If the Robie house plays with ideas of speed, it also weighs heavily on its site. It can speak of democracy, free and open, but from almost every direction it is closed or cunningly screened. It honors nature, but by meeting nature's soft shapes with its own order of sharp edges and planes.[3] Low to the ground, the house nevertheless has its primary spaces a full story above, and its sleeping rooms in an aerie. It is conceived in terms of space, and from some points of view is even transparent; but the strength of its mass remains inescapable.

When the house is considered as an abstract arrangement in mass, the *Dampfer* is plain to see [53]. Less apparent are the ways by which Wright modulates space in relation to the outer world of nature and the city. The south elevation is balanced by the porch at the west and the court wall at the east; both shield the house from mundane contact either with the street or with uncontrolled nature. The belvedere rides at high remove from the tiny traces of lawn. The north side of the house faces the world most formidably, because Wright accepts the fact that it is largely a lot-line wall, and who knows what may be built someday on the open lot [54, 55]. If the

---

[2]*Eric Mendelsohn: Letters of an Architect*, ed. Oskar Beyer (London, 1968), pp. 74–75.

[3]In his tribute to Louis H. Sullivan, *Genius and the Mobocracy* (New York, 1949), p. 55, Wright remarks that "it was my natural tendency to draw away from the mastery of his efflorescence toward the straight line and rectangular pattern, working my own rectilinear way with T-square and triangle toward the more severe rhythms of point, line, and plane." Nature sometimes got in the way; in one early and often published photograph of the Robie house, Wright has touched out the trunks of three young elm trees to keep them from interrupting the long lines of the south front.

---

[1]Wright, *Ausgeführte Bauten.*

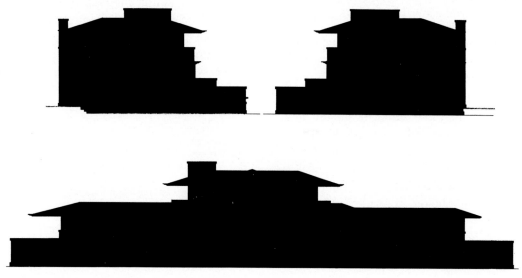

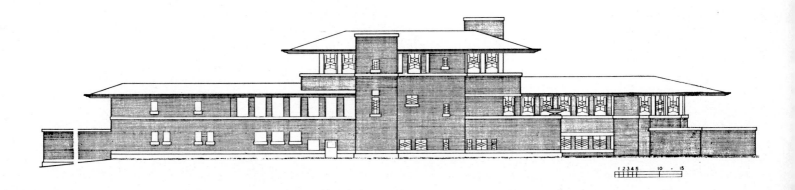

OPPOSITE, TOP: *52. Looking northeast, 1910.* OPPOSITE, BOTTOM: *53. West, east and south elevations in silhouette.* ABOVE, TOP: *54. North elevation, drawn in 1963.* ABOVE, BOTTOM: *55. Looking southeast, about 1960.*

house were essentially a matter of mass, its terraced pro-files might recall ancient step pyramids [56].[4] The inten-tions of the house, however, have nothing to do with supplication of the gods of sun or rain; the steps express instead the stages of privacy, for the house exists to be lived in [57].

But the transitions of space from outside to inside are far more subtle than silhouettes and elevations can indi-cate [58].[5] Even a small part of the house engages in a vigorous and evenly matched debate between advancing and receding planes, horizontal and vertical forces. The mysterious turns, knife-edged corners, long rhythms of repeated door and window openings, and emphatic ter-

---

[4]"I remember how as a boy, primitive American architecture—Toltec, Aztec, Mayan, Inca—stirred my wonder, excited my wishful admiration," Wright wrote in A Testament, p. 111. "Those great American abstractions were all earth-architectures: gigantic masses of masonry raised up on great stone-paved terrain, all planned as one mountain." He was also fond of the terraced massing of the Potala Palace in Lhasa, Tibet.

[5]The artist Charles Biederman has asserted that Wright did not begin with the so-called open plan: ". . . you cannot 'open' the inte-rior without first opening the exterior . . . the Wright development began on the exterior and then worked towards the interior." See his Search for New Arts (Red Wing, Minn., 1979), p. 102.

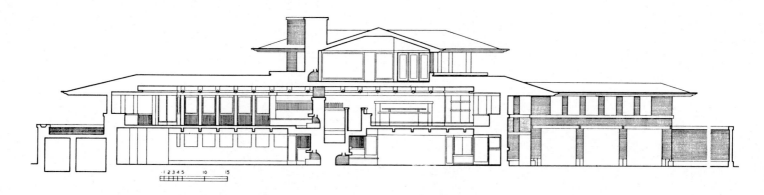

OPPOSITE: 56. *Looking northwest, about 1957. The court wall (lower right) has been reduced to the height of the garden wall. The Chicago Theological Seminary is in the background.* ABOVE: 57. *Section, looking north, drawn in 1963.* BELOW: 58. *Southwest corner, about 1957.*

minals can be compared with the most heroic moments of ordered space in Western art.[6] Wright liked to think that this extraordinary sense of counterpoint in space came to him through the toy building-elements devised by Fröbel:

> Mother learned that Frederick Froebel taught that children should not be allowed to draw from casual appearances of Nature until they had first mastered the basic forms lying hidden behind appearances. Cosmic, geometric elements were what should first be made visible to the child-mind. . . . I soon became susceptible to constructive pattern *evolving in everything I saw.*[7]

[6]Such as the Piazza San Marco in Venice, where space is held in asymmetric balance, where staggered planes enhance the turns and corners, terminals contain the long horizontal rhythms, balconies add their special drama, masonry prevails everywhere, and design is so thorough as to pattern even the pavement.

[7]Wright, A *Testament,* pp. 19–20. An epiphany of evolving constructive pattern occurs in the "Flower in the Crannied Wall" sculpture at the entrance of the Dana house, which Wright chose as the final illustration for "In the Cause of Architecture," p. 221.

ABOVE: 59. *South front, 1963.* OPPOSITE, TOP: 60. *West front, 1963. Brickwork ruined by tuckpointing.* OPPOSITE, BOTTOM: 61. *South elevation, drawn in 1963.*

Repose then comes to mean a delicate balance between forces still alert and contending. The tension is greatest in the relation of roofs to walls [59, 60]. Wright exaggerates the horizontal extensions by withdrawing their points of support. Roofs and walls thus gain an extraordinary independence.[8] When the piers are shifted nearer to the core of the house and the loads are carried by concealed cantilever beams, the nonsupporting walls become sturdy screens, folded to form pylons that stop short of the roofs and often not even below them. The

[8]Wright's development of the roof was more revolutionary than Mies van der Rohe's later discovery of the freestanding wall, and rather more subtle. "I was shocked," Mies recalled in June 1963. "One night I was working on the Barcelona pavilion and then I drew the freestanding wall. At the moment, I realized the possibilities."

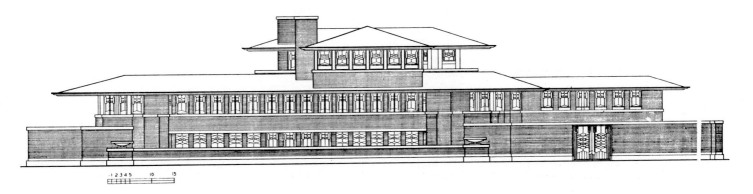

.1 2 3 4 5   10   15

corners break open.[9] These basic changes in the art of building are meant to end every implication of traditional framing and of the house as a confining box. H. P. Berlage was one of the first to understand that "that leap of roof, with its tremendous shade effect, through which its protective function (never so prominent as with Wright) found expression, is and remains the find, the fascinating piquancy of the 'tridimensional.' "[10]

Without an attic, the roofs come close to the ground to repeat the broad plane of the prairie. So do the long stretches of stone: the water table, copings and sills [61]. Windows and doors parade together, the diagonal of the steps up from the garden gets hidden, and the terminals of the long garden wall are flattened into saucers for flowers [62].[11] The long slabs of the stone trim mediate between the massing of the house and the shape of its building elements, or what Wright remembered as the slender brown bricks. In fact, their complexion is mottled of orange, red and violet, and sprinkled with black iron spots [63].[12] The bricks are finely cast and elegantly proportioned. They are laid to form continuous horizontals; the mortar beds are of ordinary cement raked one-fourth of an inch back from the face, the narrow header joints of red-colored cement brought flush to suppress the vertical breaks. Stretchers and headers form alternate courses in the mullions and narrow piers, with the middle header not quite so wide as the typical four-inch headers at each side [64].[13]

Wright compressed more and more values into the horizontal line and plane: sympathy with the prairie, repose, simplicity, intimacy of scale, broadness of vista, freedom, the easy accommodation of the flow and ebb of

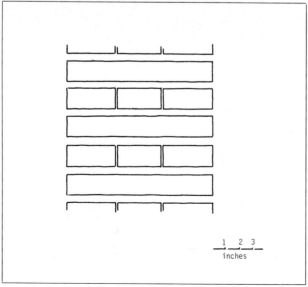

1 2 3
inches

[9]Wright had already reached an advanced stage of this device in the Yahara Boat Club project and in the Dana house. The largest of the pierlike forms in the Robie house are not the supports: the face of the pylon that shields the steps to the west porch measures 11 feet four and one-half inches, that of the planter on the inner side of the steps measures five feet two and one-quarter inches; the brick pier on which the main cantilever beam bears is only 23 inches square.

[10]Berlage, in *The Life-Work of the American Architect*, p. 82. In *Modern Architecture*, p. 70, Wright wrote: "I liked the sense of shelter in the 'look of the building.' I achieved it, I believe."

[11]The stone slab forming the lip of each urn is five feet square, or nearly four times as large as the base. The scale of the urns suggests that flowers and plants are being offered as bounteous gifts of nature.

[12]They measure one and five-eighths inches high by 11 and five-eighths inches long and four inches thick. According to Fred Robie, jr., Wright went to St. Louis to select the brick. An identical brick in the early 1960s was known as "Pennsylvania Iron Spot Roman Brick," W. B. Barnard reports.

[13]To illustrate his essay on "The Meaning of Materials—the Kiln," the *Architectural Record*, 63 (June 1928), pp. 555–561, Wright chose the Robie house, Cheney house, Larkin Building and Imperial Hotel. By 1928 he had built about 20 brick residences.

OPPOSITE, TOP: *62. Flower urn, east end of the garden.* OPPOSITE, MIDDLE: *63. Brick masonry, south front.* OPPOSITE, BOTTOM: *64. Diagram of brickwork in narrow piers.* ABOVE: *65. West front, 1910.*

front door, then making him change direction once more, a whole architectural sequence, one event after another.[15]

No concept of interior space alone could have resulted in such a transition, as Wright hinted when he wrote of the organic relation between exterior and interior.[16] To an important extent the Robie house is shaped from the outside in. The entrance withdraws from the west front, and even from the entrance walk [65, 66]. Its darkness is countered by a cheerful bed of flowers framed by the stone retaining wall [67]. The low wall also frames the entrance court, paved in concrete with a central mat of red quarry tiles.[17] Steps shielded by the brick pylon rise to the west porch, protected with an iron gate [68]. The tiles continue eastward and under the balcony, where, through the paired casement windows, the entrance hall is dimly visible [69].[18]

American life, quiet domesticity and streamlined modernity.[14] As isolated and intrusive verticals, the entrances presented a special problem. They had to be hidden. Edgar Tafel recalls the day he drove Wright and his guest Mies van der Rohe to the South Side:

> We didn't linger long in the Coonley house because Mr. Wright was anxious to have Mies see the Robie house . . . he had us look at it first from across the street, through the trees. Then we walked across to it, went left and around the end to the entrance. . . . Mr. Wright had designed an unobtrusive, almost hidden entrance. He'd planned the visitor's progression, leading him toward the building, making him turn, bringing him around to the

---

[14]See "A Home in a Prairie Town," *Ladies Home Journal*, XVIII (Feb. 1901), p. 17; *Modern Architecture*, pp. 70–71; *The Disappearing City*, p. 40; *An Organic Architecture*, p. 9; *An Autobiography*, pp. 325, 342, 349, 493; and *A Testament*, p. 219. Bruce Brooks Pfeiffer writes that Wright began having his stationery printed in a horizontal format in December 1939. From 1940 on, even contracts and agreements were prepared in horizontal format.

[15]Tafel, *Apprentice to Genius*, p. 79. So concealed is the entrance that the west elevation drawing (Fig. 30) shows no sign of it. Wright thought that the traditional American house had "an especially ugly hole to go in and come out of"; see *Frank Lloyd Wright on Architecture*, p. 178.

[16]"Now the outside may come inside, and the inside may and does go outside. They are *of* each other," Wright wrote in *An Autobiography*, pp. 337–338. The approach to Wright's studio in Oak Park had gained this kind of complexity in a remodeling of about 1906; see *The Plan for Restoration and Adaptive Use of the Frank Lloyd Wright Home and Studio* (Chicago, 1979), pp. 35–36.

[17]The flower bed is only a two-foot swath between the wall and the curb. The mat of tiles (see Fig. 25) measures six feet six inches by 22 feet, or eight tiles by 27, a rectangle slightly different from that of the site.

[18]No mullion divides the two windows; they form a single opening almost six feet wide. Their lights, 32¼ by 30 inches, are larger than those of the billiard room, which measure 31 by 28 inches.

OPPOSITE, LEFT: 66. *Entrance court, about 1938.* OPPOSITE, RIGHT: 67. *Flower bed, 1913. Isadora Wilber with her daughter Jeannette (members of the family who owned the house from November 1912 on). The Goodman house is in the background.* ABOVE: 68. *Entrance court, looking west, about 1957. Masterly coordination of tiles, concrete, stone, brick, glass, plaster soffits and copper cornices.*

69. *West casements, entrance hall.*

Chapter V
ON THE GROUND FLOOR

Robie could see from the drawings that his house would stand directly on the ground. There would not be any basement, because Wright thought a basement was an unwholesome place, and a most ugly preparation for a house:

> Invariably the damp sticky clay of the prairie was dug out for a basement under the whole house, and the rubble-stone walls of this dank basement always stuck up above the ground a foot or more and blinked, with half-windows. So the universal "cellar" showed itself as a bank of some kind of masonry running around the whole house, for the house to sit up on—like a chair.[1]

The drawings called for excavation only to make a clean break from the earth terrace to the north, to accommodate the furnace and coal rooms—four steps down from the ground floor—and to provide a pit in the first of the garage ports for working on the cars.[2]

First among the working drawings, the foundation plan is already a revelation [see 24]. It tells much about the floors above and, as Barry Byrne might say, it looks eager to introduce the elevations. It also contains those hints for geometric pattern that Wright would turn into ornament, especially in the windows and doors. The foundation plan is so articulate that it forecasts wonderful things to come; but of course the ground-floor plan is more rhythmical and developed, because of its organized openings for doors and windows [see 25]. Wright takes

from the minor vessel its only generous and potentially formal space, and makes it the entrance hall; and although the space is pierced by openings at the corners and on all sides, it maintains its integrity as a room [70].[3] Surprisingly, the hall is isolated from all the ground-story service rooms, which must be approached from the outdoors, through the garage court. With masterly skill, Wright reveals the essence of the plan by making all the main routes of access arrive at the junctures of the two vessels.

As a crossroads, the hall gives to the billiard room, the playroom, to a coat closet which in turn leads to steps up to the kitchen, to a washroom for either guests or the children coming in from play, and to the stairs to the living room and dining room. It is the formal reception space, as the plate for visiting cards makes clear, and it formally announces most of the characteristic details of the house. All of these details—the quarter-sawn oak furniture, the oak latticework screens, the portieres, the inglenook, the integrated radiators and lights, patterned rug, patterned table scarf and patterned glass in doors and windows—fit each other. Each leads to the next, and none is allowed to detract from the harmony of the whole, the *Gesamtkunstwerk*. For a house confined to a narrow city site, deprived of the full luxuriance of nature, ornament becomes all the more necessary. Wright takes from Owen Jones the idea that ornament should spring from a geometrical construction. As the

---

[1]Wright, *Modern Architecture*, p. 69.

[2]The heater-room floor has been repoured to the height of the bottom step, resulting now in a step down into the coal bin. Because the garage ports have been remodeled into offices, there is no sign today of the pit.

[3]The hall measures 19 feet, nine inches north-south by fifteen feet east-west, exclusive of the window alcove. Its ceiling is seven feet one-half inch high; the entryway clearance beneath the northwest balcony is only six feet seven and one-quarter inches.

ABOVE: 70. *Entrance hall, looking southeast, 1910. The stair runner is not yet in place.*
OPPOSITE: 71. *Entrance hall, 1916. The rounded opening for the stairwell gives it an appropriate hatchlike quality.*

melody of structure, the manifest abstract pattern of structure, ornament completes the house:

> . . . I believe that only when one individual forms the concept of the various projects and also determines the character of every detail in the sum total, even to the size and shape of the pieces of glass in the windows, the arrangement and profile of the most insignificant of the architectural members, will that unity be secured which is the soul of the individual work of art.[4]

A consistent, gracious austerity of line carries through the range of materials and subtle colors in the entrance hall to give the room that discipline through which Wright proclaims a new spirit in American life. Only a level of taste aspiring to his own can be at home. The plaque on the east wall (is it something of Mrs. Robie's?) looks merely sentimental. Soon it is gone, and other decorative sculptures have appeared; one is Wright's favo-

rite image from classical antiquity, the Winged Victory of Samothrace [71].

The first of the eight oak screens in the house perforates a small part of the wall opposite the front door to hint at the space beyond the portieres, a coat closet which the screen serves to ventilate. Built of squared and interlocked stiles and rails, the screen suggests traditional domestic architecture in Japan, where Wright had come to think of entire walls as screens.[5] Two more

---

[4]Wright, "In the Cause of Architecture," p. 164. See proposition 8 in Owen Jones, *Grammar of Ornament* (London, 1856). Also see *Frank Lloyd Wright on Architecture*, p. 236, and *An Autobiography*, p. 347. Of what he considered the ingrained human love of ornament, Wright wrote in *The Brickbuilder*, X (Aug. 1901), p. 160, that "we may be thankful that we still possess it, for back of it are probably the only instincts that make life bearable or desirable."

[5]Wright's screens, however, look more massive. The oak bars are one and five-eighths inches square, or equal to the height of the Roman brick. Their spacing is one-sixteenth inch less than their width. Wright wrote in *Organic Architecture*, p. 11, that "Japanese domestic architecture was truly organic architecture." He first visited Japan in 1905. In his 1908 essay he classified his own work according to roof types, just as traditional houses of Japan are classed. Other parallels: prominent roofs, tile roofs, broad eaves for deep shade and protection of the walls, design generated by the floor plan (the only drawing that Japanese carpenters had), use of a plan module (in Kyoto the *tatami* mat measured 3.13 feet by 6.26 feet), low lintels or trim to relate to human height, carefully filtered light, inglenooks as central symbols of hospitality, and a fondness for occult symmetries. Also see *An Autobiography*, pp. 196–200. Wright's photographs in William C. Gannett's *House Beautiful* (River Forest, Ill., 1896–1897) reveal a sensibility already nourished on Japanese art. His deep admiration for both Japanese culture and German culture must have figured in his opposition to America entering World War II.

ABOVE: *72. Entrance hall, looking northwest, 1916.* BELOW: *73. High-back chair, entrance hall. Drawn in 1967.*

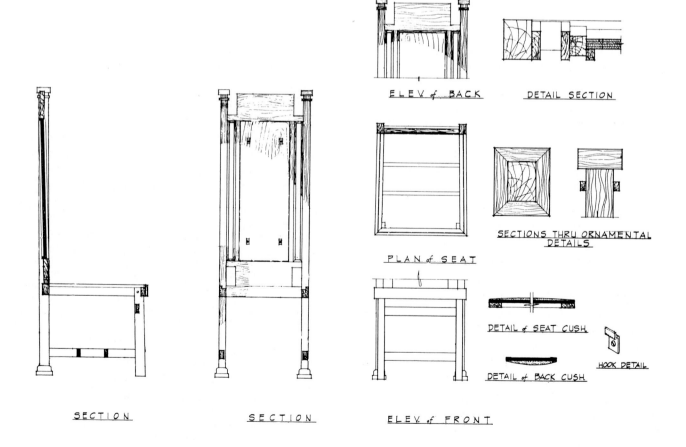

ELEV of BACK   DETAIL SECTION

SECTIONS THRU ORNAMENTAL DETAILS

PLAN of SEAT

DETAIL of SEAT CUSH

HOOK DETAIL

DETAIL of BACK CUSH

SECTION   SECTION   ELEV of FRONT

screens, at the south side of the hall, pattern the light that reaches through the walls to the fireplace alcoves of the billiard room and playroom. Sheets of glass are sandwiched into both as transparent insulation from the drafts of the hall.

On the north side of the hall, small bays for the washroom and window alcove give to the space the beginnings of a pinwheel, a shape oddly echoed by the spaces of the chimney mass and main stairwell [72]. The window alcove, sheltered from the front door and close to the radiator, forms a cozy haven. Because its built-in settle is shadowed by the balcony and hidden by the north wall, it is also a place of vantage for watching the approach of visitors.[6] The radiator is screened by casework beneath three windows grouped with unexpected symmetry to emphasize the formal tone of the reception space. Wright takes care to elevate the most common appurtenances into elements of the aesthetic whole.

No less architectural is the freestanding furniture. None of the pieces is intended as an isolated work of decorative art; all give life to the space of the room.[7] Constructed, like the casework, from what Wright called freely-marked red oak, the furniture represents a direct translation by the machine of those decisive lines and planes drawn by the architect with pencil and straightedge. Tender traces of slow handicraft are deliberately avoided.[8] Machines could make significant and virile pattern, Wright thought: the poetry of structure. Wood could speak best if only helped to be itself: "The beauty

of wood lies in its qualities as wood. . . . Why does it take so much imagination—just to see that? . . . In itself wood has beauty of marking, exquisite texture, and delicate nuances of color that carving is likely to destroy."[9]

If the top of the table is long and narrow and cantilevered to relate to the roofs of the house, the trestle supports point toward each other in a playful inversion of the prowlike salients in the plan, and the stretcher echoes the cabinetry that conceals the radiator, across the room. Even the luxurious surface of the table scarf in goat's-hair satin is tempered by an embroidered interlace of angles within rectangles that refer to the nave and aisles of the main vessel. More protestant still, the highback chair stands with back posts and legs so slightly relaxed from plumb as to appear vertical, the tilt of the back cushion only a grudging gesture toward comfort [73]. The chair back is handled again as if casework, the back foot adopts the compound curve of plinth and torus in a column base, and the finial of the back post suggests the astragal, neck and abacus of a column capital. By 1912, the entrance hall has also accommodated two side chairs of lesser scale and simpler design, and two pieces of the type George Niedecken called tabourettes, the small square tables which could also serve as stools or (as they did by 1916) as plant stands.

All the pieces retreat to the edges of the room as if yielding to the fleet of motifs advancing across the wool rug. They, too, are composed of long rectangles. The field is beige, the border a darker brown; the *Dampfer*-like motifs are of gray, red and off-white accents. "Keep in mind," an assistant of Wright's cautioned a rug dealer a few years later, when furnishing another house, "that the pattern colors shall not form holes in the background but shall come forward forming spots of brilliance."[10]

Finally, the glass. Vigorous, complex, virile, free from the sentimentality of its day, the basic design appears first in the front door [74]. Again the seeds of the pattern can be found in the plan: the two vessels, the side aisles, the prows. Only as metaphor does the glass pattern suggest a bouquet of flowers, their stems or trailing creepers.

---

[6]The alcove forecasts the inglenooks of the playroom and living room. Wright's transformation of the traditional inglenook into a vital element of spatial hierarchy is explored by Edgar Kaufmann, jr., in "Precedent and Progress in the Work of Frank Lloyd Wright," *JSAH*, XXXIX (May 1980), pp. 145–149.

[7]The furniture was built by the J. H. Bresler Co. of Milwaukee, which had a financial interest in the Niedecken-Walbridge Co. Other suppliers included Bollentin & Thompson of New York for the rugs made in Austria; F. Schumacher & Co. of New York for the spreads, pillows and table scarfs; and Johnson & Faulkner for the smaller chair fabrics.

[8]"The furniture takes the clean cut, straight-line forms that the machine can render far better than would be possible by hand," Wright said of his prairie houses. See "In the Cause of Architecture," p. 162. Edward S. Morse had observed in Japan that "wood is left in just the condition in which it leaves the cabinet-maker's plane, with a simple surface, smooth but not polished." See his *Japanese Homes and Their Surroundings* (Boston, 1885–1886, Dover reprint 20746–3), p. 111. Stickley's furniture came close to Wright's, but its emphasis on the plain and the sturdy gave it heavier membering and less graceful proportions and details. Stickley preferred to use only white oak. The furniture designed in Vienna by Josef Hoffmann had a severe simplicity unlike Wright's although equally abstract. Hoffmann had a predilection for black and white, two noncolors rather alien to wood; his furniture was lacquered. It was also hand-rubbed and smoothed with rounded corners and spherical accents.

[9]Wright, *Modern Architecture*, pp. 16–17. Trim "should be selected from straight grain for stiles, rails and running members, and from figured grain for panels and wide surfaces," Wright wrote in 1901, in "A Home in a Prairie Town."

[10]R. M. Schindler, quoted in McCoy, *Vienna to Los Angeles*, p. 36. The colors of Robie's rugs were recalled by Jeannette Wilber Scofield in a conversation of October 29, 1980; her memory is confirmed by yarn samples in the "Wool chart of rugs for Mr. Robie" in the Prairie Archives. Spencer had noted in 1900 that blues, cold greens and dead whites had no place in Wright's color schemes except as incidentals; see "The Work of Frank Lloyd Wright," p. 71.

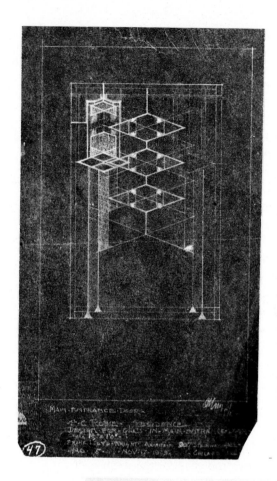

OPPOSITE, TOP LEFT: *74. Drawing for glass design of front door, November 1909.* OPPOSITE, TOP RIGHT: *75. Billiard room, looking west, 1916.* OPPOSITE, BOTTOM: *76. Billiard room, looking east, 1916. Jeannette Wilber is seated by the fireplace.* RIGHT: *77. Window details, billiard room.*

Just as the plan of the house if turned upright exhibits its greatest density in the upper register, most of the movement in the glass design is upward, in counterpoint to the horizontality of the house, so that the most intricate areas of pattern protect the privacy of those indoors. Roller shades serve at night. Wright had been eager to promote the electro-glazing process even before the turn of the century; by using copper electroplated with zinc, rather than cast lead, framing members (or cames) could be made stronger and thus thinner, or more easily varied in width to express the pattern more structurally. In the front door glass the linear pattern of the cames more than equals the intensity of the panes—of which there are more than 265, sometimes iridescent and often subtle in color.

Early in his career Wright had insisted on casements in place of double-hung windows:

> The outswinging windows were fought for because the casement window associated the house with out-of-doors—gave free openings, outward. In other words the so-called "casement" was simple and more human. In use and effect, more natural. If it had not existed I should have invented it.[11]

Because a casement window is essentially a glass door, it presents a clean field for architectural pattern, and Wright can perform variations throughout the house. He derives from the basic glass design five other patterns in the hall alone. For the alcove windows, the narrow windows above the radiator and the washroom window, there are three more simple arrangements of lozenges in clear panes. Color returns in the middle window above the radiator and in the paired doors giving to the billiard room and to the playroom.

To walk through those doors is to step from clarity into chaos [75, 76]. Never is Wright's style so apparent as when it is absent; the space and shape of the billiard room struggle to free themselves from such clutter. The plan is a better guide. It shows the billiard room conceived as a reflex of the playroom, a symmetry that requires an otherwise meaningless shape, the prow at the west end, which looks so much like the buttressed chapel of a Gothic apse. The prow forms a safety vault, and the unfinished space can be used as a wine cellar or simply for storage; yet the west end of the ground story mostly serves to support what is above. The long space of the billiard room builds a swift rhythm from its rows of windows and the modulations in its ceiling.[12] What the room loses in its blind west end, it gains from the fixed light and casement windows along the north aisle, a luxury denied to the playroom by the abutting service vessel. For privacy, the lozenge patterns now move into the lower register, because the windows are so high in the wall; and the clear panes admit as much light as possible [77]. Colored panes enrich the slender stilted figures of

---

[11]Wright, *Modern Architecture*, p. 72.

[12]The ceiling is six feet seven inches in the north aisle and in the alcove; eight feet in the nave; and six feet four inches in the south aisle. The room is 20 feet six inches wide and measures 32 feet from the door of the vault to the west edge of the alcove, or eight times the spacing of the brick mullions between the windows.

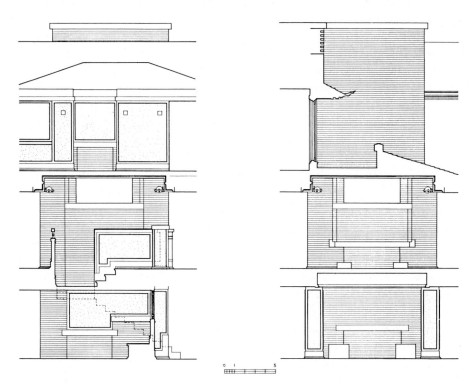

OPPOSITE, TOP: *78. Billiard-room alcove, about 1957. The lamps have been damaged and the walls painted white.* OPPOSITE, BOTTOM: *79. Fireplace elevations, looking west (left) and east, drawn in 1963.* LEFT: *80. One of the doors to the south garden.* ABOVE: *81. Garden, 1914, with Isadora Wilber.*

the French doors [78]. The fireplace, in its spare brick and stone strength, echoes the masonry outer walls of the house [79].

Through glass doors the billiard room gives onto a small concrete terrace facing the south garden [80]. In plan, the space of the garden bears a subtle relation to that of the entrance walk and court: they are staggered much like the main and service vessels. Wright must have intended for the garden a variety of flowers and shrubs, but it appears never to have been planted with much more than a swath of grass [81].[13] A long wall at

---

[13]The grassy area, eleven feet three inches at its widest, stretches 77 feet nine inches.

LEFT: 82. Garden wall, 1914. BELOW: 83. Playroom, looking west, 1916. Jeannette Wilber plays with her toys. OPPOSITE: 84. Playroom prow, looking southeast.

the south sidewalk shields this narrow space [82]. Wright and the builder had disagreed about a refinement in the wall, Barnard's son relates:

> As told to me by my father, he approached Mr. Wright during the construction and suggested that the low garden wall on the south elevation be built with a slight crown to overcome the optical illusion of concaveness. Mr. Wright rejected the suggestion. My father went ahead and built the wall with a crown anyway. A couple of hard heads, I guess.[14]

The playroom is just as barren of Wright's furnishings as the billiard room [83]. But it is redeemed by its alcoves: the friendly inglenook formed by the long and slightly cantilvered bench, and the prow, which on a fine day entices the children to the outdoors [84]. There is still another glass design. More important, Wright has transformed the projecting window bay, that casual cliché of Victorian buildings, into an integral and forceful architectural feature. The prow buds from the body of the room as its ornamental climax, and geometry meets nature on equal terms.[15]

Closer to the service vessel, an inconspicuous door opens to the court, where the children—because of Robie's fear of kidnappers—are protected by the high wall and by the extraordinary iron gates to the drive [85–87]. The gates maintain the ornamental pattern; so do even the lights of the garage doors [88]. Wright for the first time omits stables and integrates the garage ports with the body of the house. Robie thus enjoys what must be the first attached, three-car garage in the world. His son shares in this fascination with cars, and gains a miniature world of his own:

> Another memory is of the fun I had riding my tricycle out from the ground-floor playroom into the rear courtyard and back. Later, father gave me a little automobile with a real brass-trimmed radiator. Many times, in my play, I would take him from the house to work, a long and fascinating trip from the playroom to the farthest of the three garages . . . a total distance of perhaps some 50 feet. But, to me, this last garage was his office. . . . And then, later, I would pick him up and bring him home . . . father intended for the playroom and the courtyard area to be my world, and it was.

---

[14]W. B. Barnard, in a letter of October 29, 1980. As a scholar of Greek, his father must have known about such nuances in the more refined temples of antiquity.

[15]Angled details had appeared in Wright's plans since the mid-1890s, but hardly to such effect. Two of the most interesting plans prior to the Robie house are the 1903 project for the architect's studio house (fair warning that he was thinking about leaving home)

and the River Forest Tennis Club of 1906, in which the prows at each end unfortunately serve only as the women's locker room and the caretaker's quarters. The ceiling of the playroom prow in the Robie house is seven feet six inches high, still another variation. The distance from the chimney mass to the west edge of the prow windows is, again, 32 feet.

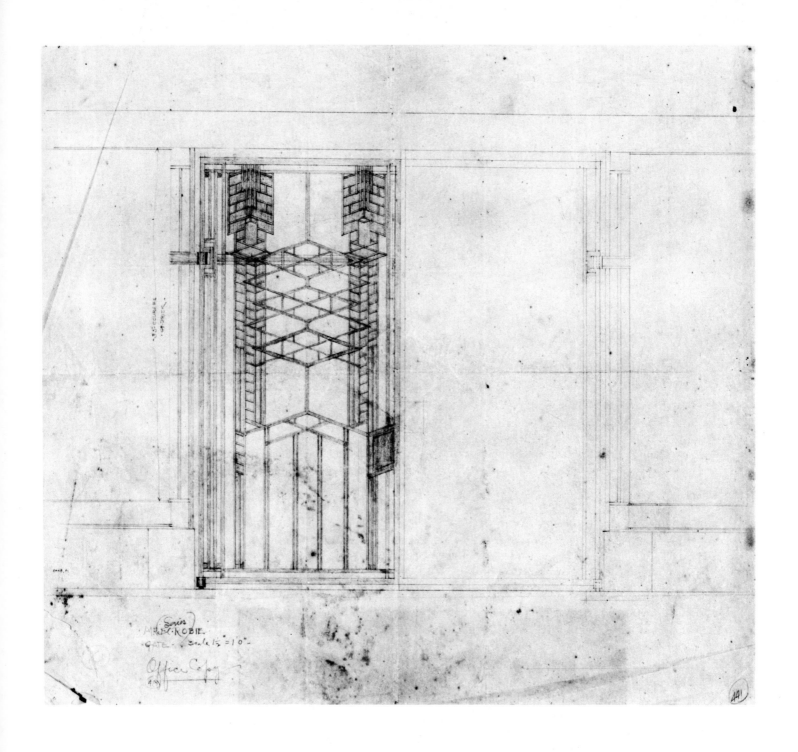

ABOVE: *85. Drawing for iron gates to garage court.* OPPOSITE, TOP: *86. Drive, about 1924, looking southeast, with Jeannette Wilber in riding habit.* OPPOSITE, BOTTOM LEFT: *87. Drive, 1918. Machine shop addition in background. Jeannette Wilber is costumed as a Christmas tree.* OPPOSITE, BOTTOM RIGHT: *88. Drawing for garage-door glass, November 1909.*

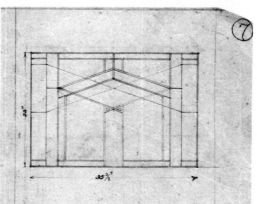

MR. F. C. ROBIE   GARAGE DOORS
SKETCH SHOWING DESIGN OF GLASS
Scale 1½" = 1'0"   NOV. 7. 1909.
Office Copy

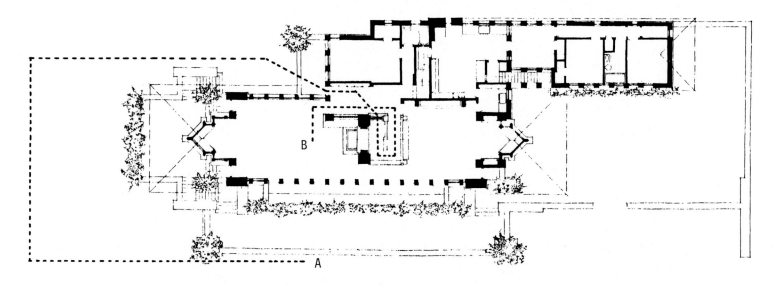

ABOVE: 89. *Approach from the sidewalk (A) to the living room (B).* BELOW: 90. *Rug plan for living room, dining room, hall and stairs.*

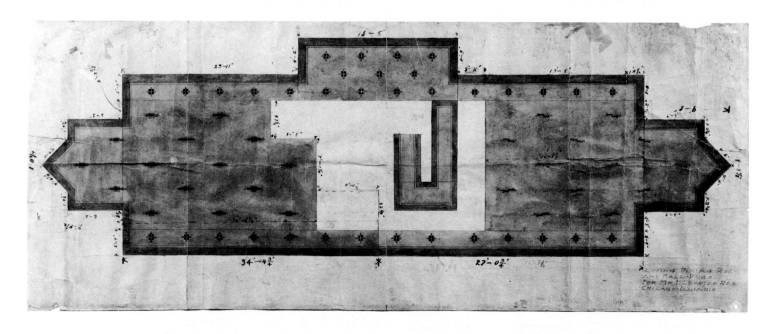

Chapter VI
INSIDE THE GREAT VESSEL

Of the 14 door and window bays which stroke across the south front of the Robie house, four belong to the dining room, two to the stairwell, one to the fireplace mass and seven to the living room. Wright also honors the living room by an approach of great deference and subtlety. Through repeated counterclockwise turns, the way to the living room condenses and reverses that long path from the south sidewalk to the entrance hall and stairwell: two complete but opposite revolutions lie between a central position outside the house and a central place indoors [89].

The stairs rise toward the south front but turn twice to the left before ending at a second and smaller hall; they fail to reach the living room. Yet the stairwell is the keyhole to the rooms of the great vessel, as is evident in the plan for rugs [90]. Now the perspectives are much more dramatically controlled by the latticed oak screens, which stand above low casepieces and stop short of the ceiling. First comes a dwarf lattice, almost ten times as long as it is tall, which rides along the casepiece of open shelves at the south wall of the stairwell; then the much taller screen above the casepiece at the west side of the dining room [91]. By breaching the chimney mass, Wright forms a spine of space along the ceiling, ribbed and continuous, to express the living room and dining room as parts of the same vessel although each retains its independence and privacy.[1] The edges of this powerful

opening are stepped as though a very large molding [92]. Conversely, the trim at the top of the stairwell is terraced with such broad strength that an ordinary molding takes on the scale and substance of structure [93]. A complex molding in copper, outdoors, defines the cornice incisively and with dignity [94]. At the entrance walk, the rhythm of curb, flower bed and retaining wall is again that of a molding. Details such as these reflect one another and the profiles of the entire house. Wright everywhere sustains the same extended cadence of line and plane. Who can say where structure ends or where ornament begins?

All four doorways from the hall at the top of the stairs can be closed with portieres [95]. In no true sense do the spaces overlap or the rooms interlock.[2] The opening to the living room is anchored by a terminal the size of a pier [96]. The casework changes to distinguish even the back of the stairwell from the back of the inglenook. The rug motif of the living room differs from that in the dining room, and both differ from the motif shared by the hall rug and aisle runners in defining the passageways.

Light from the door to the northwest balcony falls across the patterned clear-glass panes of the five tall doors to the bookcase, sunk into the north wall of the hall. Wright acknowledges the dark position of the hall

---

[1]Again, space conquers mass. In his own house of 1889, Wright placed a mirror above the fireplace to diminish mass and simulate space. The ceiling space of the Tomek house does not penetrate the chimney mass, and the wood stripping runs longitudinally.

[2]The space does not support the thesis in H. Allen Brooks, "Frank Lloyd Wright and the Destruction of the Box," JSAH, XXXVIII (March 1979), pp. 7–14. His photograph shows the living room after it has been denuded of its inglenook settle and screen, its portieres and its original furniture.

ABOVE, TOP: 91. *South aisle of first floor, looking east, 1916, with Jeannette Wilber.* LEFT: 92. *Chimney mass, southeast corner.* ABOVE, BOTTOM: 93. *Molding at southeast corner of stairwell (recent view, with tall screen gone, post at right lowered and rugs lost).* OPPOSITE, TOP: 94. *Cornice detail at the southwest corner of the main roof.* OPPOSITE, BOTTOM: 95. *First-floor hall, looking west, 1916. Bookcase at right, cases 'E' and 'D' at left. The smoker's cabinet (lower right) is from the living room.*

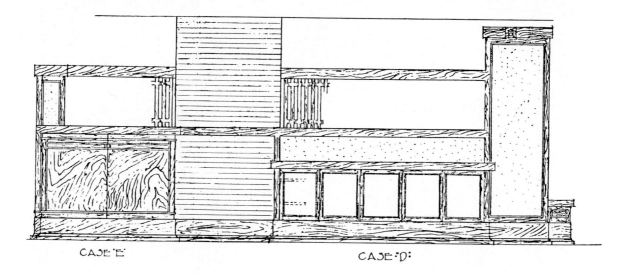

CASE 'E'   CASE 'D'

ABOVE: 96. *Drawing for south side of hall, March 1909. In a slight change, the top of case 'E' was not carried across the chimney mass.* OPPOSITE, TOP: 97. *Living room, looking west and a little north, 1910.* OPPOSITE, BOTTOM: 98. *Living room, looking west, 1916, with Isadora, Jeannette and Marshall Wilber.*

by conceiving of its ceiling as an analogue to the sky: from behind screens composed of tiny oak cubes glued between slats, incandescent bulbs cast down abstract patterns in emulation of what he once called "the mosaics of foliage."[3] The close space and dense detail of the hall can only enhance the generous and noble scale of the two great rooms.[4] To enter the living room is to be instantly impressed by its strength of character [97, 98]. Once, in an early speech at Hull-House, Wright had hinted at what he intended to accomplish in architecture:

> . . . man-made environment is the truest, most characteristic of all human records. Let a man build and you have him. You may not have all he is, but certainly he is what you have. . . . Why wonder what has become of the

grand spirit of Art that made, in times past, man's reflection in his environment a godlike thing.[5]

And so he brings to an end that artificial and pious separation down through the long history of European civilization of sacred from secular. Those who were amused to call his architecture "Horizontal Gothic" came closer to the truth than they knew.[6] Much about the Gothic cathedrals was organic in character, Wright explained in 1910, confessing an admiration that could be discerned in the living room of the Robie house, particularly its prow [99]. With its beveled grooves and edges, its pitched planes and restless moldings, the prow carries into three dimensions the most vital elements of the glass designs (they having grown from the basic angle of the prow). Bristling with salients and returns, the plan brings to mind a Gothic apse or perhaps the scheme of a fortified medieval city [100, 101].

Ten casement windows, two fixed lights and two flanking doors—all in colored glass—make the prow into a sacred grove [102]. R. M. Schindler knew exactly what Wright was about:

> Wright not only has a sense of gardens but his houses are always a piece of developed and refined environmental space—not imaginable without plants, sky and earth. This should explain to you his windows. They are not wall holes but a dissolution of the building material into a grid—leaded glass—as the ground dissolves and becomes lost in the tree branches.[7]

[3]Wright, "In the Cause of Architecture: V. The Meaning of Materials—the Kiln," the *Architectural Record*, 63 (June 1928), p. 556. Jeannette Wilber Scofield remembers the light being diffused by frosted glass, not rice paper. Spencer had noted already in 1900 the "Oriental richness and flavor" of the screened lighting in Wright's own house. The three large grilles of the Robie house hall measure about three feet east-west by six feet north-south, or close to the size of *tatami* mats.

[4]"Like everything of this architect's design," Barry Byrne wrote in recalling Wright's studio in Oak Park, "the quality of the room enveloped your being and gave a sense of becoming part of a thing of rare distinction. It was as if you were caught up in a rhythm in which you moved in grave delight." See his "Art" column in *America*, LXIX (June 1943), p. 305. The Robie living room measures 44 feet from the chimney to the point of the prow; the dining room, 30 feet six inches from the point of the prow to the posts by the casepiece at the west edge of the room. Both rooms are 20 feet seven inches wide.

[5]Wright, *Modern Architecture*, pp. 8, 12.
[6]Wright, *Modern Architecture*, p. 71.
[7]As quoted in McCoy, *Vienna to Los Angeles*, p. 131. Wright's abstraction of "The Fruit-Bearing Tree" figured in the frontispiece of *The House Beautiful* in 1896–1897; a tree of life appeared in the ornamentation of the columns by the entry to his Oak Park studio, and a tree of life was prominent in his glass designs for the Darwin D. Martin house of 1904–1906.

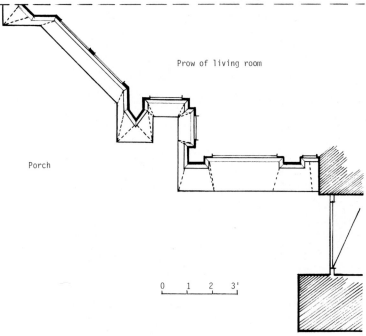

Prow of living room

Porch

0 1 2 3'

ABOVE: 99. *South side of living-room prow.* LEFT: 100. *Half-plan diagram of living-room prow. Broken lines show bevels in stone.* BELOW: 101. *Living-room prow, looking east.* OPPOSITE: 102. *Inside the prow, looking northwest, about 1957.*

The glass designs flower in the upper register to cast sunlit splashes of color deeper into the room and to form a screen, for privacy, above that of the walls and parapets [103, 104]. Many of the little panes are iridescent, and their hues run through a rich chain of gold, violet, turquoise, rose, reddish-brown, brown and green. In one of the window designs it is possible to sense a standing figure, or signs of Indian arrowheads and feathering [105, 106].[8] Robie was delighted:

> The setup was wonderful for stained-glass windows, the very small design, clean-cut, which would in the sun's rays . . . shed the colorings of the leaded glass over the floors of the rooms, and particularly on the coverings and materials and furniture, which Mr. Wright . . . was designing and contracting for. . . . The special furnishings, which were provided under Mr. Wright's artistic ability and knowledge from the Niedecken Company at Milwaukee, included some tables, chairs and a hand-woven wool rug from Austria, embodying some designs that were in keeping with the glass in the windows, which were going to throw the sunlight over the major central section, in color . . . it seemed *alive*, because of the movement of the sun. . . . So, altogether, we had a constantly shifting pattern of color, figurations, and the comfort of the very heavy rug.

The paradox is this: when at last the room is reached, there are invitations everywhere to move toward the edges and look back outdoors. The north wall opens through five large casement windows, the prow turns and folds into a crown of glass; and the south wall builds a most subtle rhythm: first the very narrow fixed light, then a casement window that opens by the well through the balcony floor, and finally the flight of French doors, 12 pairs in a continuous row [107–109].[9] Wright dis-

---

[8]Wright embellished his first office with Indian statuettes by Hermon MacNeil, and MacNeil's "Dancing Hopi" was stationed at the entranceway of the W. H. Winslow house, his first major independent commission. In 1924, Eric Mendelsohn found Wright prepared to go hiking in dress that included bark shoes, a long staff, gloves and a tomahawk: "something Indian about it," Mendelsohn wrote. See his *Letters of an Architect*, p. 73.

[9]The light wells not only enframe the balcony but express its cantilever. They follow a design change shown in pencil on the builder's set of blueprints.

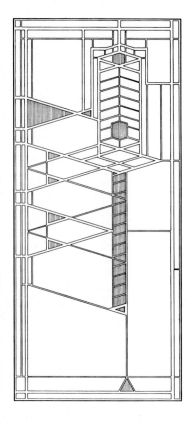

OPPOSITE, TOP LEFT: 103. *Paired casements, north side of the prow.* OPPOSITE, TOP RIGHT: 104. *Glass design for paired casements, drawn in 1963.* OPPOSITE, BOTTOM LEFT: 105. *Smaller casement, north side of the prow.* OPPOSITE, BOTTOM RIGHT: 106. *Smaller casement from inside, looking south.* ABOVE, LEFT: 107. *Fixed light in south aisle, only four and one-half inches wide.* ABOVE, RIGHT: 108. *Window above the west light well in the balcony.* RIGHT: 109. *Doors to the south balcony, about 1957. The storm sash is fitted from inside as part of the trim.*

solves an entire wall into a thin and vibrant screen of patterned glass. The floor is extended through this wall-as-a-window to become a long and narrow balcony [110–112].[10] Its attractions are fresh air and sun, a command of the street, the long view toward the Midway Plaisance and the pleasure of a high place on the deck of the *Dampfer*. Robie's son spoke of the vista:

> One of the nicest things about the house was the beautiful view to the south. From our raised living room and dining room we could look out over a two-block vacant area to the Midway Plaisance. . . . Father and mother remember enjoying watching the skaters from that distance . . . the central portion of the Midway was flooded in the wintertime, and people by the hundreds came out . . . to ice-skate.

Indoors, the perspectives toward the fireplace enjoy the full dynamic of the plan [113, 114]. The rug motif is composed of a rose-colored rectangle flanked by 12 small green squares and extended at both ends. The long runner of the south aisle slips past the chimney mass, in a special passage to the dining room. Night lights, screened by patterned oak grilles, stretch along the soffits of both aisles, and lamps within milky globes are cantilevered into the upper space of the nave as if blossoms from the ribbing, which springs from the south doors and returns at the north windows, expressing a plastic continuity of wall and ceiling. So the ceiling becomes a sheltering bower, a source of patterned light. Only narrow planes of wall are left. They are finished darker, to relate not to the ceiling but to the warm field of the rugs.[11]

---

[10]Wright is after a narrow and dynamic ledge of space (the balcony space measures five feet six inches by 47 feet nine inches), and cares less about structural expression, which is impure in the sense that a heavy parapet of brick trimmed in stone seems to float above an open garden. The stones hung along the lower edge are eight feet eight inches long. But the alternative of a parapet faced in stucco and trimmed with wood would have conflicted with the basic character of the house.

[11]Maya Moran has shown me a wall surface in the Tomek house finished to a warm honey-brown and richly textured and scumbled into color harmonies somewhat like those of dried leaves. In the Robie house, Wright may have used beeswax to give the walls the patina of age. Beeswax as a finish for lime-plaster walls is described by Ji Cheng in the *Yuan Ye*, a Ming dynasty text completed in 1634. Wright was fascinated with Oriental tonalities.

The step in scale from floor and wall and ceiling to the freestanding furniture of the room is rendered almost imperceptible by the large and vigorously structured table lamp. It repeats in miniature the idea of a sheltering ceiling and source of friendly light. Two early studies show how much attention was paid to the table lamps [115, 116]. In the study for the larger lamp, the elaboration of the connections between the shade and posts recalls the extreme articulation of wood joinery in the traditional architecture of Japan; the shade in the study for the smaller lamp looks like the traditional rice-straw hat, broad and conical, worn by peasants in southeast Asia as protection from sun and rain. Neither lamp appears to have been made. Instead, a replica of a lamp designed for the Dana house in Springfield finds its place at the end of the library table, becoming a crucial element of the room. On the smaller table, across from the built-in settle of the inglenook, the Robies have evidently placed an Art Nouveau lamp from their apartment. The table itself is from Wright's design, although it differs from the study for a small trestle table, intended perhaps for another room [117].

Most of the chairs must have looked to Robie like old friends; a Craftsman-style rocker was prominent in the living room of the apartment on Cornell Avenue. Wright's oak chairs often came close in spirit to Gustav Stickley's catalogue furniture, and George Niedecken frequently ordered Craftsman pieces in working on other interiors. But the refinements in the Robie chairs are quickly remarked: the feet are curved, the sides are paneled and enhanced by rhythmic enframements, the blocks between arms and front posts are decisively angled, the backs paneled, and the back posts kicked into ears. Hardly so successful, the "all-over upholstered chairs" (as Niedecken called them) conceal their structure and sacrifice that strength and clarity characteristic of the rest of Wright's furniture. Their satin finish refers instead to the embroidered table scarfs. A small smoker's cabinet is stationed toward the northwest corner of the room. Nearer to the hall comes the most extraordinary member of the ensemble: a monumental paneled settle with arms so widely cantilevered that they serve as side tables. At the inglenook the built-in cushioned settle forms a retreat to the primal warmth of the fireplace, one

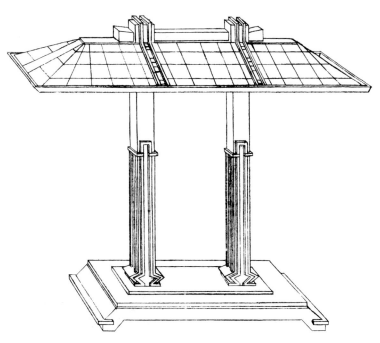

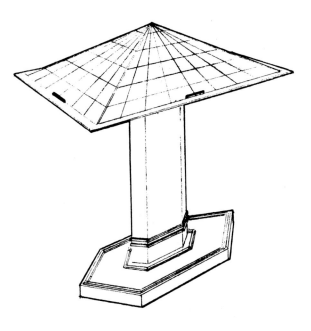

OPPOSITE, TOP: *114. Living room, looking east, 1910.* OPPOSITE, BOTTOM LEFT: *115. Study for living-room lamp.* OPPOSITE, BOTTOM RIGHT: *Study for small lamp.* ABOVE, LEFT: *117. Study for trestle table.* ABOVE, RIGHT: *118. Living-room inglenook, April 1915, with Jeannette Wilber as a gnome.* RIGHT: *119. South aisle, looking east, 1916, with Jeannette Wilber.*

of those moments in the rhythm of life that Wright revered [118]: "It refreshed me to see the fire burning deep in the masonry of the house itself."[12] The inglenook opens to the south and to the aisle that leads to a much different space [119].

Were it not for the orientation of the majestic dining table, guarded by its tall chairs, the fact that the central space of the dining room is wider than it is long would be hard to sense [120]. This unexpected counterpoint in plan is gently ornamented by the crossed table scarfs, so lovingly considered that the shorter scarf is pointed at each end to express the axis of the prows. Four of the six legs tucked far under the table invert the angles of the prows. Close by the corners, the pillars can shift outward

---

[12]Wright, *Modern Architecture*, p. 70.

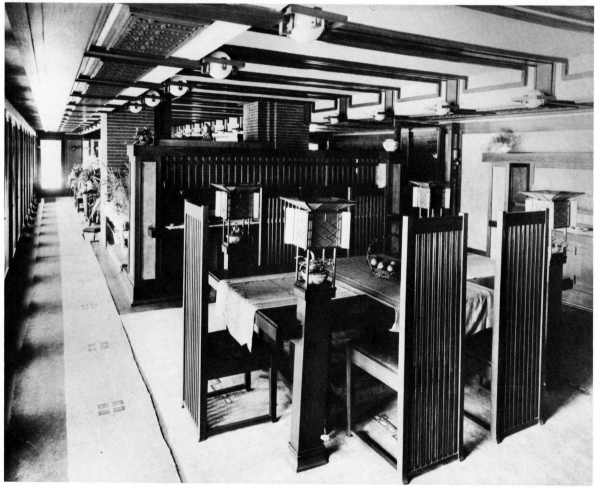

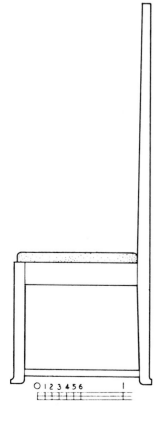

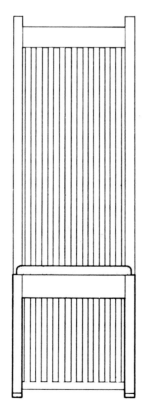

OPPOSITE, TOP: *120. Dining room, looking northeast, 1910.* OPPOSITE, BOTTOM: *121. South aisle and dining room, looking northwest, 1916.* ABOVE: *122. Dining room, looking northwest, 1916.* LEFT: *123. Dining-room chair, drawn in 1963.*

to accept extensions; they serve also to carry the concentric ceramic planters and the curious stilted lanterns with double shades in patterned glass. This forest of posts and finials marks a space of high ceremony, a place so ornamented there is no call for anyone to say grace.

The tall chairs speak to the screen above the casework at the west edge of the room [121–124].[13] The horizon-

---

[13]The dining-room chairs measure 52 and three-eighths inches high, and their square spindles are half as wide as the stiles in the oak screens. Ledgers of the Niedecken-Walbridge Co. show that the dining-room ensemble was constructed over several months; the lampshades were completed February 19, 1910, and a pottery company was paid on May 28 for the "4 small bowls with inner bowls." The table as reconstructed and exhibited in the Smart Gallery of the University of Chicago has the lamp wiring extended through holes in the ceramic bowls. The high-back chairs in Wright's own dining room of 1895 had spiral spindles; he replaced them later with square ones. He also remodeled the back feet of his own chairs to make them flare outward, writes Donald G. Kalec, director of research and restoration at the Wright home and studio.

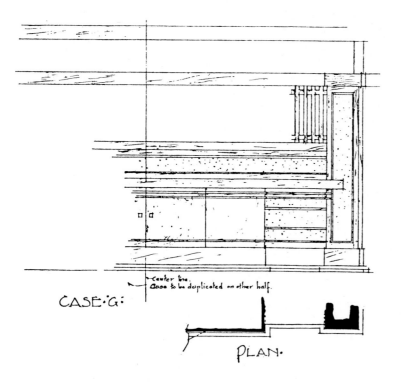

CASE·G:

PLAN·

LEFT: *124. Elevation and plan for casepiece at the west side of the dining room, March 1909.* BELOW: *125. Elevations for sideboard (case 'H'), breakfast nook and prow, with half-plan for ceiling moldings, March 1909.* OPPOSITE, TOP: *126. Dining room, looking southeast, 1916.* OPPOSITE, BOTTOM: *127. Drawings for the breakfast table.*

tals of the casepiece race between sturdy terminals to suggest the south elevation of the house, and now the rug motif plays on the relation of the two vessels in plan. Appropriately, the most beautiful of all the casepieces is the sideboard built along the north wall to correspond to the last three bays of the south front of the house [125]. It takes the idea of the cantilever to a high level of abstraction, satisfying Wright's intention to create interiors as "intimate expressions or revelations of the exteriors."[14]

Morning light falls on the square table that is turned to fit so tidily into the breakfast alcove [126, 127]. The rotated square is quickly repeated by the grille of the

[14]Wright, "In the Cause of Architecture," p. 163.

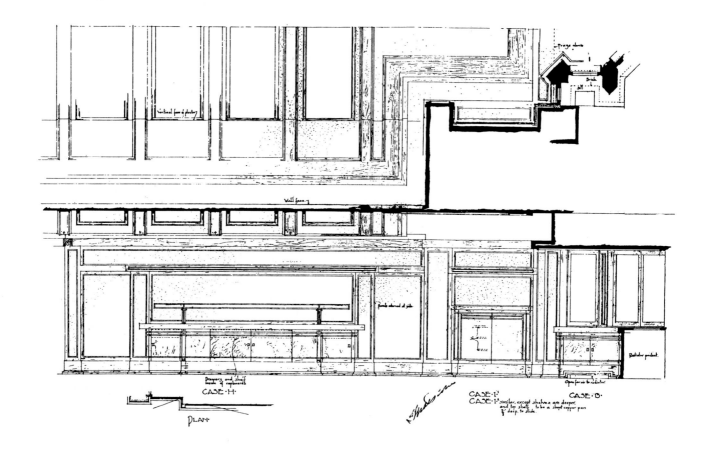

CASE·H

PLAN·

CASE·I·
CASE·I·

CASE·B·

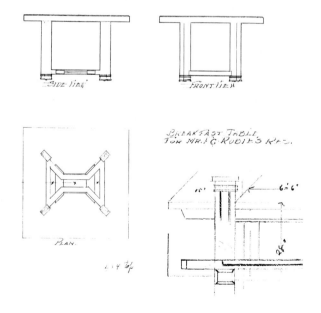

ventilator in the prow ceiling [128].[15] At this end of the vessel, the prow is partly retracted into the body of the room, and has fewer windows; but they are enlivened with varied designs [129, 130]. The basic casement design appears again in the window above the east well of the balcony [131]. The sources of incandescent light are the same as those in the living room [132–134]. At close range, the wall-mounted fixture unfolds squares within squares and the feathering that once more suggests Indian arrows [135].[16] From below, the plan derives from one of Wright's earliest and most favored motifs, the circle within a square [136]. It finds its echo by leaping outdoors to the flower urns [137, 138].

[15]The ventilation channels today could easily accept all the ductwork necessary for central air-conditioning, Calvert Audrain reports. Another rotation occurs in the one-inch-square brass rods that hold the eight pairs of portieres (one pair in the entrance hall, four in the first-floor hall, two at the doors to the west porch and one at the door from the dining room to the balcony overlooking the court).

[16]Wright updated the entry to his studio in Oak Park by adding what were evidently extra lamps from the Robie house.

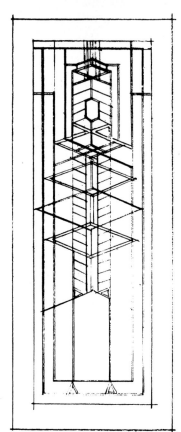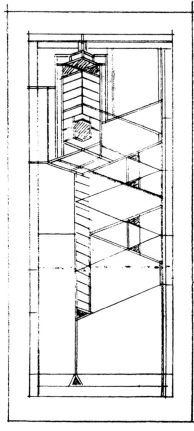

TOP, LEFT: *128. Grille of the vent in the dining-room prow.* LEFT: *129. Drawings for glass designs in the dining-room prow.* TOP, RIGHT: *130. Casement at the southeast corner of the dining-room prow.* ABOVE: *131. Casement above east light well, with Jeannette Wilber.*

TOP: *132. Typical lamp in the first-floor nave. Heavier members of the ceiling moldings project one and three-quarters inch.* ABOVE: *133. Typical light grille in the aisle soffits. A frosted-glass panel is missing.* RIGHT: *134. Typical wall-mounted brass lamp. The door is to the southeast balcony, overlooking the courtyard.*

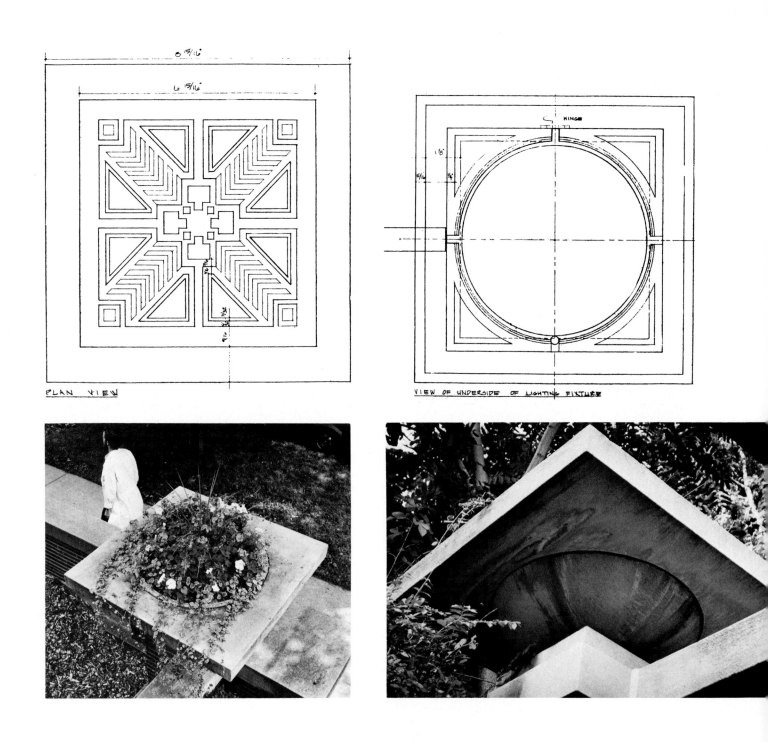

PLAN VIEW

VIEW OF UNDERSIDE OF LIGHTING FIXTURE

TOP, LEFT: *135. Plan of the top of a wall-mounted lamp, drawn about 1967.* TOP, RIGHT:
136. Plan of the bottom of a wall-mounted lamp, drawn about 1967. BOTTOM, LEFT: *137. Top
of the flower urn at the west end of the garden.* BOTTOM, RIGHT: *138. Underside of the flower
urn at the northwest balcony.*

Chapter VII
THE ROOMS BEYOND

After the intensity and splendor of the dining room, the rest of the house retires to that spare, quiet elegance introduced by the entrance hall. Situated directly above the hall, the guest room is the last place in the house to be characteristically and completely furnished by Wright through the services of George Niedecken [139]. By comparison with most of the sleeping rooms designed by Wright in his early years, the space is large; but it is oddly proportioned and awkwardly lighted.[1] Robie, according to his son, had asked for the room:

> My father could foresee the time when his parents might live with us, so he asked Mr. Wright to include a guest room and bath on the main living room–dining room floor. This Mr. Wright did. So, later, after my grandfather Robie's sudden death, my grandmother did come to live with us. She was a semi-invalid, but was very happy here, because she had access to the living part of the house without any stair-climbing.

The handsome rug design depends on the broadened border, where long and vessel-like shapes rest within harbors formed from rotated squares. In the design of the dresser and double bed, the same simple strength informs even the caps of the mirror posts, which come to a point like the prows, and the angled embroidery of the pillow cases and spread [140]. One of the side chairs is matched by a sewing rocker; both have a high back-splat that descends in abstract rigor all the way to the

139. *Guest room, looking west, 1916. The table is not of Wright's design.*

stretchers [141].[2] The other style of side chair matches those in the living room. Convenient to the guest room, the bathroom is carefully screened from the main living spaces and thoughtfully fitted with a fixed interior pane

---

[1]The room measures 19 feet one inch east-west by 11 feet four inches north-south; the corridor ceiling drops to about six feet eight inches as though to prepare one for this long space lighted only at the west end and not shaded from the evening sun, the most unpleasant source of heat during summers in the Middle West.

[2]The side chair stands 40½ inches high. There were about 600 chairs of this general type (though not so refined) in the restaurant of the Larkin Building, writes Jack Quinan of the State University of New York at Buffalo.

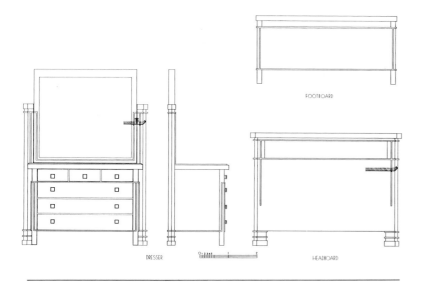

FOOTBOARD

DRESSER　　　　HEADBOARD

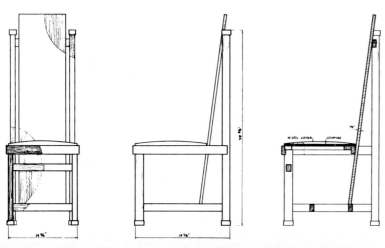

of frosted glass to pass on the north light from the patterned casement to the service stairs [142].

In a change from the drawings of March 1909, a doorway gives from the corridor to the kitchen, or what Wright liked to call the "working department" [143].[3] Here the casework is quite ordinary; only the wood stripping and the glass design by the gas range speak with any style [144]. Part of the east wall is taken by a huge icebox, supplied through an opening at the service entry [145]. Simple casement windows light the sink and drains, and fixed interior panes borrow light from the servants' sitting room, causing a playful ambiguity of indoors and out.[4] The servants retire to bedrooms provided with patterned casements and with the pleasures of a long flower box above the garage ports [146]. To enhance the small space in each room, the ceilings rise toward the roof.

A ceiling again rises tentlike in the stairwell to the bedroom belvedere, where the wood trim and the patterned casements greet nature with a straight-lined, lovely geometry [147, 148]:

> . . . in a structure conceived in the organic sense, the ornamentation is conceived in the very ground plan, and is of the very constitution of the structure. . . . It is fair to explain the point, also, which seems to be missed in studies of the work, that in the conception of these structures they are regarded as severe conventions whose chief office is a background or frame for the life within them and about them. They are considered as foils for the foliage and bloom which they are arranged to carry, as

[3]Wright, "A Small House with 'Lots of Room in It,' " *Ladies Home Journal*, XVIII (July 1901), p. 15. Wright took much more care with the appearance of his kitchens as servants disappeared from middle-class life in America. Contrary to the first-floor plan as drawn for the Historic American Buildings Survey, the indented southwest corner of the Robie kitchen, which forms a cranny by the stairs to the bedroom belvedere, must have been original. The H.A.B.S. drawings fail to show the interior fixed light of the guest bathroom, the light trough over the outdoor stairs to the kitchen and the bookcase in the first-floor hall. They also err as to the height of the court wall, which was eight and one-half feet tall, and in various of the glass designs as shown in the elevation drawings.

[4]This thirst for light also resulted in the opening at the juncture of the two roofs to light the 14 steps from the court to the kitchen entry; see Figs. 26, 27.

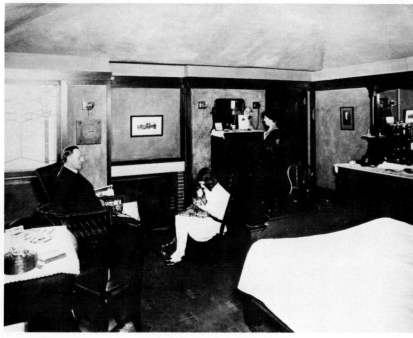

OPPOSITE, LEFT: *146. Casement in the west servant's bedroom.* OPPOSITE, RIGHT: *147. Stair hall in the belvedere, looking north.* LEFT, TOP: *148. Casement and lamp detail, belvedere stair hall.* LEFT, BOTTOM: *149. Master bedroom, looking northwest, 1916. A room never graced with Wright's furniture. Again, the Wilbers.* ABOVE: *150. Detail of casements, southwest corner of the master bedroom.*

well as a distinct chord or contrast, in their severely conventionalized nature, to the profusion of trees and foliage with which their sites abound.[5]

By describing the highest floor of the house as the belvedere, a place in command of a beautiful view, Wright emphasizes the positive aspect of his elimination of the attic. The plan, at first, recalls a Greek cross; but the four arms are not of the same length or weight. Centered three bays east of the chimney mass, the belvedere builds a bridge between the vessels below. Its spaces are parallel to those of the vessels, and the master bedroom faces southward like the living room and dining room [149].[6] The prismatic effect in the plan of 1909 comes from the broken lines expressing the folds in the

---

[5]Wright, *Ausgeführte Bauten.*

[6]The common interpretation of the belvedere as a major cross-axis is not accurate. The interior dimensions: master bedroom, 23½ feet east-west by 17 feet six and one half inches north-south; northwest bedroom, 15 feet five and one-half inches square; northeast bedroom, 16 feet two inches east-west by 11 feet three and one-half inches north-south.

OPPOSITE, TOP: *151. Northwest bedroom, 1916. Alien furniture and curtains.* OPPOSITE, BOTTOM: *152. Casement in the closet, northwest bedroom.* ABOVE: *153. Northeast bedroom, 1916. Only the bed is Wright's furniture. Jeannette Wilber is at her desk.*

ceiling, which often occur out-of-phase with the roof ridges; yet the illusion of a room rising to the roof is perfect [150]. H. P. Berlage found particular delight in the uppermost spaces of Wright's prairie houses:

> . . . many of the rooms on that floor have the roof for a ceiling. This, together with the radically projected eaves, gives the rooms a quiet tone. . . . I had the impression of an extraordinary intimacy, and only with great effort could I tear myself away from those rooms.[7]

Besides the amenities of a fireplace and private bath, the master bedroom has two extensions: to the east, a dressing room with mirrored wardrobes; and, to the west, a long closet with a wall safe and patterned-glass door to a tiny balcony. The melange of furniture in the room by

1916 indicates that it never came under Niedecken's control, just as the wool rug, although evidently made for the room, shows a confusion of motifs that betrays a hand other than Wright's.

High above Woodlawn Avenue, the northwest bedroom enjoys a view all its own [151]. As in the other bedrooms, drawers for clothing and linens are sunk into spaces beneath the outdoor flower box; the same is true of the radiators.[8] Even the closet has its glass design [152]. In all the bedrooms the wall openings that address the flower boxes are divided by three-inch rails into casement windows over small fixed lights. Seen from the street, the rails help express the openings as windows, rather than doors onto diminutive balconies, and they repeat the horizontal line in the highest reaches of the house. Indoors, they discourage children from trying to climb out. The last bedroom, at the northeast, is the smallest [153]. Most of its windows look east to the early morning light, like those in the bathrooms [154].

---

[7]Berlage, "The New American Architecture (1912)," in *The Literature of Architecture*, ed. Don Gifford (New York, 1966), p. 612.

[8]Similarly, hundreds of file cabinets were sunk into the walls below the windows of the Larkin Building.

154. Casements in the bathroom next to the northeast bedroom.

Chapter VIII
THE MOST IDEAL PLACE IN THE WORLD

In the spring of 1909 there must have been days when everything looked right to Fred C. Robie. Very soon he saw everything go wrong. Moments of hope and light and beauty are as fragile as a butterfly's wings. In 1958, when Robie thought back to the time of his father's death, on July 18, 1909, his voice turned weak:

I was told later by an associate that I was with him seven minutes, during which time I held his hand—or, rather, he held onto life—until he could tell me, "Fred, every dollar I want paid that I owe. Will you do it?" I agreed to. The next few days were rather hectic. Some care of my mother was required. . . . The business end of both his properties and mine coasted along . . . probably three or four weeks while I was flying from one place to another and from one lawyer's office to another's to get his attorneys and my attorneys in alignment for a complex process of liquidation. . . . My father had—based on his friendships—he had on my note borrowed many thousands of dollars at different times. . . .

So I was not such a big fellow after all. . . . I presume my father at times had borrowed, and had been on paper for me, as much as $300,000 to $400,000. And not a thought was given by these men. They had known him for years, 20 or 30. They knew he was a two-fisted guy, and, somewhat acquainted with me, hoped I'd follow in his steps. . . . Well, the debts were paid—at least, I think, it was 93 or 97 percent. Approximately $1 million was involved, and Dun & Bradstreet gave me a very nice letter having to do with the confirmation of my father's name and mine. And I received much congratulation and well wishes from my former creditors.

I had ended at approximately 30, with no darn interest except to be a great manufacturer. . . . The one completed product that was absolutely mine was a son, the first child.

It took almost two years to sell the businesses and settle most of the debts, Robie recalled. During the same time his marriage was disintegrating. Lora Robie left the house in April 1911, taking both children. She filed for divorce in January 1912, and it was granted March 1.[1] Robie had sold the house in December 1911 to David Lee Taylor, president of the Taylor-Critchfield Co., an advertising agency. Taylor was tired of commuting to the city from the north suburb of Wilmette. He presented the new house to his wife as a Christmas gift. "He wanted the whole works, so we made a deal that I was to walk out with only my clothes and personal effects," Robie recalled. "And I did. I got out of there."[2]

Phillips Taylor, then ten years old, can remember the house well:

[1] *Lora H. v. Frederick C. Robie*, gen. no. 12s291946, Superior Court of Cook Co., Ill. Mrs. Robie alleged infidelity and produced testimony that Robie and a friend left the Chicago Athletic Club one night to visit a house of ill repute on S. Dearborn, only a block from the notorious Everleigh Club, which had just closed its doors. Soon after the divorce, Robie moved to New York, where he failed as an automobile salesman. He returned to Chicago, was unable to find work, and later moved to Detroit. In July 1912 Mrs. Robie and the children moved from Chicago to Springfield, Ill.

[2] See the *Chicago Sun-Times*, November 18, 1958, p. 18. Robie at the same time sold his motorcycle-manufacturing business to Arnold, Schwinn & Co.: "The motorcycle business is dependent on good roads," he recalled, "and the roads then weren't good." Taylor's note to his wife read: "To Dear Momma/ Our $50,000 house/ Pop." One piece of furniture, in fact, had been removed from the house—"Sunny" Robie's bed. He kept it the rest of his life and it is now in the collection of the Smart Gallery. A price list sent to Taylor by George Niedecken on January 6, 1912, indicates that Taylor ordered a few more of the furnishings intended for the house, including the andirons in the billiard room. In the ledger of "doubtful accounts," Robie is listed as late as December 1916 as still owing Niedecken $1,000. The wonder is that he furnished as much of the house as he did.

One of my first recollections [is] of a "walk-in" vault at the end of the first-floor room facing Woodlawn. The vault door was locked—we did not have a key or combination, so a locksmith was called. As he worked, all stood around speculating—was it full of wine, art, guns or even money? But when the door swung open, it was empty!

On the second floor, the distance from the end of the dining room to the end of the living room (which was pointed like the prow of a boat, as is evident from the exterior, causing many of the observers to feel that the original builder was a former sea captain) was about 100 feet or so, giving a distance of twelve round trips down the Fifty-eighth street side and back on the opposite side of about half a mile, which was a pretty fair track for four healthy youngsters. (My two youngest brothers—David, a year old, and Gerard, who was born in the Robie house—didn't participate.)

The dining room chairs were at a fixed table . . . The chairs were tall, with absolutely straight backs that set a record for unequalled agony of sitting.

There was a central vacuum cleaner throughout the house, a telephone intercom system, [and a] heating system that was sort of separate from the house in that it could not be entered except from a separate entrance. The window planters were so designed that they could all be watered simultaneously with one valve—which didn't

work. One of the showers had a series of pinpoint sprays that would come at you from every direction.

When we left, mother took along a lamp . . . a custom-made chair, and a large copper-lined humidor. We have no idea of what eventually happened to them.[3]

David Lee Taylor died in October 1912. His wife sold the house in November and moved the family back to Wilmette [155].

All the remaining years that the house was a single-family residence, it belonged to Marshall Dodge Wilber, who with his wife Isadora and their daughters, Marcia and Jeannette, had been living at 5708 Madison (now Dorchester) Avenue, less than four blocks away. Since 1890 Wilber had been treasurer of the Wilber Mercantile Agency, a commercial reports and collections company headed by his uncle. He kept a steam yacht, the *Cornelia*, at the foot of Randolph Street, only a brisk walk from his office in the Ashland Block, and he had served in 1904 and 1905 as commodore of the Chicago Yacht

---

[3]Letter of November 19, 1980. Signs of the watering system and the vacuum system still exist. Tim Samuelson writes that the latter was typical of large buildings of the time, and that once it was proposed to build a central vacuum system for all of Chicago.

Club [156]. No doubt he appreciated the *Dampfer* aspects of the house more than anyone else [157].

Mrs. Wilber kept diaries and ledgers in which she recorded much about life in the house, starting with an entry of November 18, 1912: "Mar'l bought red Robie's house on Woodlawn & 58th St. . . . 3:30 P.M. 6 others wanted it."[4]

After they moved in, on December 3, the Wilbers came to know the house as essentially four long rooms. They called the living room the "parlor," and the billiard room the "music room." The servants' rooms were occupied by a cook who was paid $8 a week and a "2nd girl" who was paid $7 a week. A man came to water and cut the grass (such as it was), to clean the porches twice a week and the entrances every day, and to attend the coal-fired boiler. He charged $15 a month. Wilber didn't want a chauffeur, because he liked to drive; later, he became an amateur aviator, and his wife kept an electric car. At the east end of the garage, Wilber built a machine shop for working on his boat motors. Otherwise, he and his wife loyally kept the house intact. And that was no easy task.

During their first winter, Mrs. Wilber noted with alarm that the temperature indoors sometimes dropped into the lower 50s. The three great flower urns outdoors had to be covered to prevent ice damage, and by April she had put three men to work tuckpointing the walls. She also engaged a man she called "Shonkair" (Shankar?), who measured all the rugs and runners at 237 square yards and charged $75 to clean them. Mrs. Wilber, whose peculiar talent it was to whistle classical music to a piano accompaniment, received dressmakers almost daily. Once she had 200 guests for a luncheon. At her evening parties the ceiling lights glowed most romantically: "It looked like moonlight all through the house," her daughter said not long ago. Jeannette Wilber also liked the mirrored doors of her mother's wardrobe; she could arrange them so as to count 36 reflections of herself. She recalls, too, that the family dined in the breakfast alcove unless there were guests.

When the university built Ida Noyes Hall in 1915–1916 as a center for women students, the vista toward the Midway was much reduced. Even so, the distance from the south balcony of the house to the north wall of the gymnasium was 470 feet and the landscaping was greatly improved. During these years, Marcia Wilber was gravely ill; she died in November 1916, at

---

[4]Jeannette Wilber Scofield and Peter Kountz kindly allowed me to study the fragments from Mrs. Wilber's diaries.

OPPOSITE: *155. The Taylor family, about 1915, after returning to Wilmette. Ellen Taylor sits in a chair from the Robie living room; the lamp is from the same source. From left: Phillips Taylor, Winfield Taylor, Gerard Taylor (holding his mother's hand), Ellsworth Taylor, Whitman Taylor and David Lee Taylor, jr.* ABOVE, TOP: *156. The Cornelia. About 110 feet long, beam 15 feet, draft six feet, 450 h.p., it slept nine below and a crew of five.* ABOVE, BOTTOM: *157. Looking northeast, about 1914. Marcia Wilber (left) with Jeannette Wilber.*

158. *Looking northeast, 1925. Isadora Wilber's electric car.*

only 25. A series of sepia-toned photographs was soon made inside the house as a memorial and record of the surviving members of the family. Now the house seemed even colder: "bitter cold," Mrs. Wilber wrote on the last day of 1916, as she recorded the temperature of her room at 58. A pipe had burst in the dining-room wall two years earlier, and in the summer of 1916 repairs had been made to three windows and to the roof. One day in 1917, Mrs. Wilber complained that the house was "like a tomb." At the end of that year she recorded 44 degrees, evidently a record low. She had been paying $9.85 for a ton of coal. Even the conversion to an oil-fired furnace, in 1919, failed to solve the problem; in 1920 she was spending as much as $31 a week for heating-oil, at nine cents a gallon. A new furnace, in 1921, proved more satisfactory.

Impromptu visits from Wright no doubt encouraged the Wilbers. "I remember him well, his cape flying, and his hair," Jeannette Wilber Scofield said recently. "He said, 'This is the best example of my work.' " Her mother mentioned the first visit from Wright in her diaries:

Frank Lloyd Wright called 4:30 P.M. said he was the architect and asked if he could see the house. I showed him all through 3 floors. Asked if he could bring Madam Noel in (left her in car with her daughter). I replied, certainly—but we talked of other things & then he thought there was not time . . . he wants to buy the house to live in & build glass [?] extension on S. first floor.

Was he thinking seriously of returning to Chicago? Was he daydreaming of an annex that could serve as his studio? Mrs. Wilber mentions another visit in a second fragment, also undated: ". . . here about ¾ of an hour—wore solid brown suit. Said he would like to live here, but hadn't much money." Then a visit of May 31, 1924: "Frank Lloyd Wright & Mr. Zoblaier [?] and little daughter Nanien—came aft. in big car—I came down and went over first & second floor with them—told them how I loved every part of the house."

Soon enough Wilber was in his sixties and not in good health; his daughter was grown up. The directors of the Chicago Theological Seminary, which had moved in 1923 from the North Side to a site directly across Woodlawn Avenue, were keeping an acquisitive eye on the Robie house, the Goodman house and the empty space between them [158]. Wilber sold the house to the seminary on June 9, 1926. All the furnishings, except for one linen bedspread, which his wife took from the guest

159. South front, 1941.

160. The Dampfer, *about 1950.*

room as a memento, stayed with the house.[5] Although the house served for some years as a dormitory, the directors of the seminary remained primarily interested in its site. By 1941 the place looked nearly overgrown [159]. Wright heard that the house was about to be demolished, and he instigated a campaign to "protest against such vandalism in the name of property convenience."[6] The house survived. By 1950 much of the interior had been stripped or crudely altered. The outer shell lived on, a

dark and mysterious presence and an embarrassing challenge to all the falsely Gothic buildings of the university and the seminary [160].

In March 1957, Wright led another battle for preservation. The seminary had kept quiet for more than a year its plans for new dormitories on the site of the house. Wright now was nearly 90 years old. "It all goes to show the danger of entrusting anything spiritual to the clergy," he said. Once more the house was rescued, but only as an inauthentic fossil.[7]

Fred C. Robie, long retired, was living in an apartment in Cleveland. One day he was asked about the house he had built in Hyde Park. He looked back to a happier time. "I think it's the most ideal place in the world," he said.[8]

[5]The seminary paid $90,000 for the house. A furniture inventory listed an overstuffed chair (?), living-room table, three easy chairs, one cabinet table, three tabourettes, one dining-room table, nine dining-room chairs, one breakfast table, one hall table, two hall chairs, one dresser, one rocker, one side chair, one fireside cushion covered in goat's hair, three living-room and hall table scarfs, three dining-table covers, eight pairs of portieres, one set of andirons, four fern bowls, two rockers, one davenport, one double bed, two straight chairs, two hall chairs, twelve Austrian hand-tufted rugs, six stair and hall Austrian rugs and three Austrian stair rugs. In 1967 the seminary gave to the university what furnishings were still in storage; only 46 items were listed. A revised list prepared at the Smart Gallery in 1979 includes items not designed by Wright, items from other Wright buildings, items separated into parts, and even a number to which no item is assigned.

[6]Wright, in a letter of March 20, 1941, to Mrs. Julius Weil (a daughter of Dankmar Adler). Wright wrote Mrs. Weil that the house was "a source of world-wide architectural inspiration." Among those who attended a meeting of the Committee for the Preservation of Frank Lloyd Wright's Robie House on April 25, 1941, were Mies van der Rohe, Ludwig Hilberseimer and Walter Peterhans, all of the Illinois Institute of Technology and all formerly of the Bauhaus in Dessau and Berlin, and, from the University of Chicago art department, Ulrich A. Middeldorf, who in Munich had been a student of Heinrich Wölfflin's—a fair indication of the German affinity for the house.

[7]"If you want history validated, what do you go to?" Wright asked in Chicago on November 21, 1957. "Architecture. Now, of course, we started in Chicago to have an architecture of our own, and the Robie house is one of the cornerstones of that architecture." See *Chicago,* Jan. 1983, p. 126. William Zeckendorf bought the house for $125,000 in August 1958 and used it temporarily as an office for Webb & Knapp, his development firm. He planned to give the house to the National Trust for Historic Preservation, but in February 1963 gave it instead to the university. The house was remodeled for the Adlai E. Stevenson Institute of International Affairs; later, it served as an office for university development, and most recently has been the office of alumni affairs. In the years since World War II the house has been violated in every way, so that almost nothing about it is right (or Wright).

[8]*Chicago Sun-Times, loc. cit.* Fred Robie, jr., said he saw Wright at the Hotel Sherman in Chicago in October 1956: "He asked about father, and commented, 'A good house, for a good man.' "

INDEX

Pages indicated by *italics* contain an illustration of the subject only.